FIG HEEL™

WRESTLING FIGURE

ENCYCLOPEDIA

All figure photography, front, spine and back cover photos shot by Matthew Goldberg (@mbg1211)
Fig Heel & Matthew Goldberg utilize Extreme Sets Pop-Up Dioramas available at extreme-sets.com.

See a mistake in any of the information provided? Let us know in an e-mail to:
FigHeel@gmail.com

First Edition: July 2025

10 9 8 7 6 5 4 3 2 1

TABLE OF CONTENTS

MATTHEW GOLDBERG PHOTOGRAPHY

Like most things in life do, The Ultimate Wrestling Figure Checklist has evolved. What started as quite literally a page-by-page list soon turned into a full color guide with photos and even some contributions from former and current WWE Superstars Matt Cardona and Xavier Woods. In a few short years, this simple tool climbed the Amazon Bestseller list to #1 and grew into something even bigger...

Welcome to Fig Heel's Wrestling Figure Encyclopedia!

If you are reading this, I can only assume you are a member of the incredible community of wrestling figure collecting! Whether you stick to one specific company or graze across the plane, this tool will assist in keeping track of everything you have, want and need!

The Wrestling Figure Encyclopedia has been split into two separate volumes: Modern (which focuses on releases between 2010 to present day) and Vintage (focusing on all releases pre-dating 2010 – coming soon)! With a vast array of collectors only collecting vintage or only collecting modern releases, this allowed me to include more pictures and more entries while also keeping the pricing down.

So, how do you navigate The Wrestling Figure Encyclopedia? First, each wrestling promotion has their own section in the book and each section is then divided into micro sections for each toy company that manufactured product. Each toy company is then split up by individual toy line and each toy line is split up by series and lineup to make navigating a little simpler.

On the right side of each list, you will find two "empty" boxes. The first of the two boxes is the "MOC Box" and the second is the "Loose Box". This is how you will categorize your collection. There are two ways you can fill in these boxes: you can simply "check" them off when a figure is acquired or you can use a pencil to write in the current market value of the item and periodically update it. Keeping record of value will help in maintaining an overall value of your collection for personal and insurance purposes. A new feature for WWE Elites and Ultimates is the inclusion of event date which the performer wore the gear the figure depicts. Refer to the diagram below for a visual example:

WWE ELITE COLLECTION SERIES 118 (2025)		MIB	LOOSE	VALUE
SMACKDOWN – 6/28/2024	Jacob Fatu			
WRESTLEMANIA 22	John Cena (Collector's Edition)			
SMACKDOWN – 5/17/2024	Nia Jax (Standard – White)			
SMACKDOWN – 5/10/2024	Nia Jax (Chase – Red)			
SMACKDOWN – 5/17/2024	Solo Sikoa			
BACKLASH 2024	Tama Tonga			
SMACKDOWN – 5/31/2024	Tonga Loa			

Lastly, I see this more than a checklist. Consider this a coffee table book you can leave out in your man cave as anyone who picks it up is sure to get a blast of nostalgia. Now this is where the fun begins – taking inventory and filling in what you have, want and need. Enjoy!

WWE

WORLD WRESTLING ENTERTAINMENT

WWE BASIC SERIES 1 (2010)	1 OF 1,000	MOC	LOOSE	VALUE
Batista				
Big Show				
Evan Bourne				
John Cena				
Kofi Kingston				
Triple H				

WWE BASIC SERIES 2 (2010)	1 OF 1,000	MOC	LOOSE	VALUE
CM Punk				
Jack Swagger				
Kane				
Mark Henry				
Rey Mysterio (Dark Blue)				
Rey Mysterio (Light Blue)				
Vladimir Kozlov				

WWE BASIC SERIES 3 (2010)	1 OF 1,000	MOC	LOOSE	VALUE
Chris Jericho				
The Great Khali				
Mickie James				
Randy Orton				
Shelton Benjamin				
The Undertaker				

WWE BASIC SERIES 4 (2010)	1 OF 1,000	MOC	LOOSE	VALUE
Dolph Ziggler				
Goldust				
Matt Hardy				
MVP				
Shawn Michaels				
William Regal				

WWE BASIC SERIES 5 (2010)	1 OF 1,000	MOC	LOOSE	VALUE
Batista				
The Hurricane				
John Cena				
Melina				
Mike Knox				
R-Truth				

WWE BASIC SERIES 6 (2010)	1 OF 1,000	MOC	LOOSE	VALUE
Big Show				
Drew McIntyre				
Edge				
Kelly Kelly				
The Miz				
Ted Dibiase				

WWE BASIC SERIES 7 (2010)	1 OF 1,000	MOC	LOOSE	VALUE
Kofi Kingston				
Michelle McCool				
Rey Mysterio				
Sheamus				
The Undertaker				
Yoshi Tatsu				

WWE BASIC SERIES 8 (2011)	MOC	LOOSE	VALUE
Chris Masters			
Christian			
Kane			
Kofi Kingston			
Finlay			
Maryse			

WWE BASIC SERIES 9 (2011)	MOC	LOOSE	VALUE
Evan Bourne			
Jack Swagger			
JTG			
Mark Henry			
Natalya			
Rey Mysterio			

WWE BASIC SERIES 10 (2011)	MOC	LOOSE	VALUE
Dolph Ziggler			
John Cena			
Kofi Kingston			
Triple H			
Wade Barrett			
Zack Ryder			

WWE BASIC SERIES 11 (2011)	MOC	LOOSE	VALUE
Big Show			
Daniel Bryan			
Eve			
Sheamus			
Skip Sheffield			

WWE BASIC SERIES 12 (2011)	MOC	LOOSE	VALUE
Alberto Del Rio			
Evan Bourne			
John Morrison			
Randy Orton			
Rey Mysterio			
Wade Barrett			

WWE BASIC SERIES 13 (2012)		MOC	LOOSE	VALUE
#01	Rey Mysterio			
#02	Vickie Guerrero			
#03	John Morrison			
#04	R-Truth			
#05	Ezekiel Jackson			
#06	The Undertaker			

WWE BASIC SERIES 14 - ROYAL RUMBLE HERITAGE (2012)		MOC	LOOSE	VALUE
#07	Bret "Hit Man" Hart			
#08	Shawn Michaels			
#09	Goldust			
#10	Rey Mysterio			
#11	John Morrison			
#12	Alberto Del Rio			

WWE BASIC SERIES 15 (2012)		MOC	LOOSE	VALUE
#13	Layla			
#14	Kofi Kingston			
#15	John Cena			
#16	Wade Barrett			
#17	Brodus Clay			
#18	Kane			

WWE BASIC SERIES 16 - WRESTLEMANIA HERITAGE (2012)		MOC	LOOSE	VALUE
#19	Ultimate Warrior			
#20	John Cena			
#21	Eddie Guerrero			
#22	Triple H			
#23	The Undertaker			
#24	Jack Swagger			

WWE BASIC ACTION FIGURES SERIES 17		MOC	LOOSE	VALUE
#25	Rey Mysterio			
#26	Dolph Ziggler			
#27	Zack Ryder			
#28	The Miz			
#29	Alex Riley			
#30	Mark Henry			

WWE BASIC SERIES 18 - RAW SUPERSHOW (2012)		MOC	LOOSE	VALUE
#31	Kelly Kelly			
#32	Sin Cara			
#33	Hunico			
#34	CM Punk			
#35	John Cena			
#36	Cody Rhodes			

WWE BASIC SERIES 19 (2012)		MOC	LOOSE	VALUE
#37	Hornswoggle			
#38	Evan Bourne			
#39	Kofi Kingston			
#40	Justin Gabriel			
#41	Jinder Mahal			
#42	Randy Orton			

WWE BASIC SERIES 20 - GLOBAL SUPERSTARS (2012)			MOC	LOOSE	VALUE
#43	CANADA	Natalya			
#44	MEXICO	Rey Mysterio			
#45	JAPAN	Yoshi Tatsu			
#46	USA	John Cena			
#47	IRELAND	Wade Barrett			
#48	UK	Sheamus			

WWE BASIC SERIES 21 (2012)		MOC	LOOSE	VALUE
#49	Beth Pheonix			
#50	R-Truth			
#51	The Miz			
#52	Mason Ryan			
#53	Jack Swagger			
#54	Big Show			

WWE BASIC SERIES 22 (2012)		MOC	LOOSE	VALUE
#55	Booker T			
#56	Mark Henry			
#57	Chris Jericho			
#58	Christian			
#59	John Cena			
#60	Zack Ryder			

WWE BASIC SERIES 23 (2012)		MOC	LOOSE	VALUE
#61	Rey Mysterio			
#62	Alicia Fox			
#63	Hunico			
#64	Santino Marella			
#65	Triple H			
#66	Kane			

WWE BASIC SERIES 24 (2013)		MOC	LOOSE	VALUE
#01	John Cena			
#02	CM Punk			
#03	Zack Ryder			
#04	Drew McIntyre			
#05	Sheamus			
#06	AJ			

WWE BASIC SERIES 25 - RAW SUPERSHOW (2013)		MOC	LOOSE	VALUE
#07	Big Show			
#08	Brock Lesnar			
#09	Randy Orton			
#10	The Miz			
#11	Eve			
#12	David Otunga			

WWE BASIC SERIES 26 - WRESTLEMANIA HERITAGE (2013)		MOC	LOOSE	VALUE
#13	"Macho Man" Randy Savage			
#14	Shawn Michaels			
#15	The Undertaker			
#16	Kane			
#17	Mark Henry			
#18	Daniel Bryan			

WWE BASIC SERIES 27 (2013)		MOC	LOOSE	VALUE
#19	Cody Rhodes			
#20	Kofi Kingston			
#21	Wade Barrett			
#22	Ryback			
#23	Brodus Clay			
#24	Antonio Cesaro			

WWE BASIC SERIES 28 (2013)		MOC	LOOSE	VALUE
#25	Rey Mysterio			
#26	R-Truth			
#27	Heath Slater			
#28	Sin Cara			
#29	Tensai			
#30	Damien Sandow			

WWE BASIC SERIES 29 - WORLD CHAMPIONS (2013)		MOC	LOOSE	VALUE
#31	Ultimate Warrior			
#32	Eddie Guerrero			
#33	Stone Cold Steve Austin			
#34	Big Show			
#35	John Cena			
#36	CM Punk			

WWE BASIC SERIES 30 (2013)		MOC	LOOSE	VALUE
#37	The Miz			
#38	Hornswoggle			
#39	Santino Marella			
#40	Sheamus			
#41	Daniel Bryan			
#42	AJ Lee			

WWE BASIC SERIES 31 (2013)		MOC	LOOSE	VALUE
#43	Kane			
#44	R-Truth			
#45	Zack Ryder			
#45	Zack Ryder (Alternate Head)			
#46	Rosa Mendes			
#47	Wade Barrett			
#48	Alberto Del Rio			

WWE BASIC SERIES 32 - ROYAL RUMBLE (2013)		MOC	LOOSE	VALUE
#49	Chris Jericho			
#50	The Rock			
#51	Randy Orton			
#52	John Cena			
#53	Ryback			
#54	Antonio Cesaro			

WWE BASIC SERIES 33 (2013)		MOC	LOOSE	VALUE
#55	Big Show			
#56	Dolph Ziggler			
#57	The Great Khali			
#58	CM Punk			
#59	Tamina Snuka			
#60	Dean Ambrose			

WWE BASIC SERIES 34 (2013)		MOC	LOOSE	VALUE
#61	John Cena			
#62	The Miz			
#63	Rey Mysterio			
#64	Sin Cara			
#65	Ricardo Rodriguez			
#66	Brodus Clay			

WWE BASIC SERIES 35 (2014)		MOC	LOOSE	VALUE
#01	Kane			
#02	Damien Sandow			
#03	Daniel Bryan			
#04	Triple H			
#05	Cody Rhodes			
#06	Jinder Mahal			

WWE BASIC SERIES 36 (2014)		MOC	LOOSE	VALUE
#07	CM Punk			
#08	Big E Langston			
#09	Christian			
#10	Jack Swagger			
#11	Fandango (Clean Shaven)			
#11	Fandango (Stubble)			
#12	Kaitlyn			

WWE BASIC SERIES 37 - WRESTLEMANIA HERITAGE (2014)	MOC	LOOSE	VALUE
#13	Mr. Perfect			
#14	Batista			
#15	Roman Reigns			
#16	Randy Orton			
#17	Zeb Colter			
#18	Ryback			

WWE BASIC SERIES 38 (2014)	MOC	LOOSE	VALUE
#19	Chris Jericho			
#20	Dolph Ziggler			
#21	Vickie Guerrero			
#22	Sheamus			
#23	The Miz			
#24	Kofi Kingston			

WWE BASIC SERIES 39 (2014)	MOC	LOOSE	VALUE
#25	Bray Wyatt			
#26	Rob Van Dam			
#27	Justin Gabriel			
#28	John Cena			
#29	Christian			
#30	Heath Slater			

WWE BASIC SERIES 40 - GLOBAL SUPERSTARS (2014)			MOC	LOOSE	VALUE
#31	CHICAGO	CM Punk			
#32	MEXICO	Alberto Del Rio			
#33	SAN DIEGO	Rey Mysterio			
#34	PUNJAB, INDIA	The Great Khali			
#35	LONG ISLAND	Zack Ryder			
#36	TORONTO	Edge			

WWE BASIC SERIES 41 (2014)		MOC	LOOSE	VALUE
#37	Daniel Bryan			
#38	Santino Marella			
#39	Cesaro			
#40	Drew McIntyre			
#41	Bray Wyatt			
#42	Fandango			

WWE BASIC SERIES 42 (2014)		MOC	LOOSE	VALUE
#43	Natalya			
#44	Batista			
#45	El Torito			
#46	Big Show			
#47	Roman Reigns			
#48	Sin Cara			

WWE BASIC SERIES 43 (2014)		MOC	LOOSE	VALUE
#49	Mark Henry			
#50	Eva Marie			
#51	Rob Van Dam			
#52	John Cena			
#54	Dolph Ziggler			
#55	Rey Mysterio			

WWE BASIC SERIES 44 (2014)		MOC	LOOSE	VALUE
#53	Kane			
#56	Big E			
#57	Randy Orton			
#58	Seth Rollins			
#59	Titus O'Neil			
#60	Goldust			

WWE BASIC SERIES 45 (2015)		MOC	LOOSE	VALUE
#01	Triple H			
#02	Chris Jericho			
#03	Mankind			
#04	The Miz			
#05	Ricky "The Dragon" Steamboat			
#06	Daniel Bryan			

WWE BASIC SERIES 46 (2015)		MOC	LOOSE	VALUE
#08	Big Show			
#09	Kofi Kingston			
#10	Bad News Barrett			
#11	Jerry "The King" Lawler			
#12	Batista			

WWE BASIC SERIES 47 (2015)		MOC	LOOSE	VALUE
#13	Alicia Fox			
#14	Rusev			
#15	Brock Lesnar			
#16	Kane			
#17	Christian			
#18	Cesaro			

WWE BASIC SERIES 48 - WRESTLEMANIA HERITAGE (2015)		MOC	LOOSE	VALUE
#19	Ric Flair			
#20	Hulk Hogan			
#21	Brie Bella			
#22	John Cena			
#23	Booker T			
#24	Randy Orton			

WWE BASIC SERIES 49 (2015)		MOC	LOOSE	VALUE
#25	Ryback			
#26	Bray Wyatt			
#27	Roman Reigns			
#28	Bret Hart			
#29	Bo Dallas			
#30	Emma (Long Legs)			
#30	Emma (Short Legs)			

WWE BASIC SERIES 50 (2015)		MOC	LOOSE	VALUE
#31	Daniel Bryan			
#32	Adam Rose			
#33	Seth Rollins			
#34	Goldust			
#35	Summer Rae			
#36	Sami Zayn			

WWE BASIC SERIES 51 (2015)		MOC	LOOSE	VALUE
#37	Dolph Ziggler			
#38	Dean Ambrose			
#39	Stardust			
#40	Stephanie McMahon			
#41	Stone Cold Steve Austin			
#42	Heath Slater			

WWE BASIC SERIES 52 (2015)		MOC	LOOSE	VALUE
#43	John Cena			
#44	Chris Jericho			
#45	The Miz			
#46	Nikki Bella			
#47	Mark Henry			
#48	Adrian Neville			

WWE BASIC SERIES 53 (2015)		MOC	LOOSE	VALUE
#49	Brock Lesnar			
#50	The Rock			
#51	Triple H			
#52	Damien Mizdow			
#53	AJ Lee			
#54	Tyler Breeze			

WWE BASIC SERIES 54 (2015)		MOC	LOOSE	VALUE
#55	Roman Reigns			
#56	The Rock			
#57	Rusev			
#58	Big Show			
#59	Dolph Ziggler			
#60	Tyson Kidd			

WWE BASIC SERIES 55 (2015)		MOC	LOOSE	VALUE
#60	Sting			
#61	John Cena			
#62	El Torito			
#63	Kane			
#64	Randy Orton			
#65	Bray Wyatt			
#66	The Undertaker			
#67	Charlotte			

WWE BASIC SERIES 56 (2016)		CHASE	MOC	LOOSE	VALUE
RAW	Dean Ambrose				
NXT	Hideo Itami				
RAW	John Cena				
DIVAS	Naomi				
LEGENDS	Ultimate Warrior				
SMACKDOWN	Xavier Woods				

WWE BASIC SERIES 57 (2016)		CHASE	MOC	LOOSE	VALUE
SMACKDOWN	Big Show				
RAW	Daniel Bryan				
SMACKDOWN	Erick Rowan				
NXT	Finn Balor				
DIVAS	Paige				
RAW	Ryback				

WWE BASIC SERIES 58 (2016)		CHASE	MOC	LOOSE	VALUE
SMACKDOWN	Bad News Barrett				
NXT	Bayley				
LEGENDS	Edge				
SMACKDOWN	Fandango				
NXT	Kevin Owens				
DIVAS	Lana				
LEGENDS	Paul Orndorff				
SMACKDOWN	Stardust				
RAW	The Undertaker				

WWE BASIC SERIES 59 (2016)		CHASE	MOC	LOOSE	VALUE
RAW	Bray Wyatt				
DIVAS	Eva Marie				
LEGENDS	Honky Tonk Man				
SMACKDOWN	R-Truth				
NXT	Sasha Banks				
SMACKDOWN	Sheamus				
LEGENDS	The Iron Sheik				
RAW	Triple H				

WWE BASIC SERIES 60 (2016)		CHASE	MOC	LOOSE	VALUE
RAW	Brock Lesnar				
RAW	John Cena				
NXT	Kalisto				
SMACKDOWN	Kofi Kingston				
SMACKDOWN	Luke Harper				
RAW	Randy Orton				
DIVAS	Renee Young				
RAW	Seth Rollins				

WWE BASIC SERIES 61 (2016)		CHASE	MOC	LOOSE	VALUE
SMACKDOWN	Big E				
RAW	Dean Ambrose				
RAW	Dolph Ziggler				
NXT	Finn Balor				
RAW	John Cena				
DIVAS	Natalya				
NXT/SD	Neville				
NXT	Sami Zayn				
SMACKDOWN	Zack Ryder				

WWE BASIC SERIES 62 (2016)		MOC	LOOSE	VALUE
DIVAS	Becky Lynch			
SMACKDOWN	Roman Reigns			
RAW	Sin Cara			
LEGENDS	Sting			
SMACKDOWN	The Miz			

WWE BASIC SERIES 63 (2016)		CHASE	MOC	LOOSE	VALUE
RAW	Alberto Del Rio				
NXT	Baron Corbin				
RAW	Paul Heyman				
SMACKDOWN	Rusev				
SMACKDOWN	Ryback				
RAW	Seth Rollins				
LEGENDS	Sid Justice				
RAW	The Undertaker				

WWE BASIC SERIES 64 (2016)		MOC	LOOSE	VALUE
NXT	Apollo Crews			
RAW	Braun Strowman			
RAW	Brock Lesnar			
SMACKDOWN	Dolph Ziggler			
RAW	John Cena			
RAW	Lana			
SMACKDOWN	Xavier Woods			

WWE BASIC SERIES 65 (2016)		MOC	LOOSE	VALUE
SMACKDOWN	Kane			
NXT	Emma			
RAW	Kevin Owens			
RAW	Roman Reigns			
NXT	Samoa Joe			
SMACKDOWN	Sheamus			
RAW	The Rock			

WWE BASIC SERIES 66 (2016)		MOC	LOOSE	VALUE
SMACKDOWN	Albertio Del Rio			
SMACKDOWN	Big Show			
RAW	Daniel Bryan			
RAW	Dean Ambrose			
RAW	Paige			
RAW	Roman Reigns			
SMACKDOWN	Tyler Breeze			

WWE BASIC SERIES 67 (2017)		CHASE	MOC	LOOSE	VALUE
SMACKDOWN	Cesaro				
SMACKDOWN	Goldust				
RAW	JBL				
RAW	John Cena				
SMACKDOWN	Luke Harper				
WOMEN'S	Naomi				
RAW	Randy Orton				
SMACKDWON	Xavier Woods				

WWE BASIC SERIES 68A (2017)		CHASE	MOC	LOOSE	VALUE
SMACKDOWN	Bo Dallas				
RAW	Braun Strowman				
RAW	Brock Lesnar				
NXT	Dana Brooke				
LEGENDS	Diamond Dallas Page				
NXT	Finn Balor				
SMACKDOWN	Kalisto				
RAW	Neville				

WWE BASIC SERIES 68B (2017)		CHASE	MOC	LOOSE	VALUE
RAW	AJ Styles				
NXT	Alexa Bliss				
RAW	Chris Jericho				
RAW	Seth Rollins				
LEGENDS	Sting				
NXT	The Rock				

WWE BASIC SERIES 69 (2017)		CHASE	MOC	LOOSE	VALUE
SMACKDOWN	Bray Wyatt				
SMACKDOWN	Dean Ambrose				
SMACKDOWN	John Cena				
RAW	Sami Zayn				
WOMEN'S	Sasha Banks				
LEGENDS	Sgt. Slaughter				
WOMEN'S	Tamina				
RAW	Triple H				

WWE BASIC SERIES 70 (2017)		CHASE	MOC	LOOSE	VALUE
SMACKDOWN	Apollo Crews				
WOMEN'S	Brie Bella				
NXT	Carmella				
LEGENDS	Ric Flair				
RAW	Roman Reigns				
NXT	Samoa Joe				
RAW	The Rock				
LEGENDS	Ultimate Warrior				

WWE BASIC SERIES 71 (2017)		CHASE	MOC	LOOSE	VALUE
NXT	Austin Aries				
SMACKDOWN	Baron Corbin				
WOMEN'S	Charlotte				
RAW	Finn Balor				
SMACKDOWN	John Cena				
RAW	Seth Rollins				
LEGENDS	The Undertaker				

WWE BASIC SERIES 72 (2017)		CHASE	MOC	LOOSE	VALUE
SMACKDOWN	Dean Ambrose				
SMACKDOWN	Dolph Ziggler				
WOMEN'S	Nia Jax				
RAW	Sheamus				
NXT	Shinsuke Nakamura				
SMACKDOWN	Zack Ryder				

WWE BASIC SERIES 73 (2017)		MOC	LOOSE	VALUE
SMACKDOWN	AJ Styles			
RAW	Big E			
RAW	Cesaro			
RAW	Kevin Owens			
RAW	Seth Rollins			
RAW	Triple H			

WWE BASIC SERIES 74 (2017)		MOC	LOOSE	VALUE
WOMEN'S	Bayley			
SMACKDOWN	John Cena			
LEGENDS	Kane			
RAW	Neville			
RAW	Roman Reigns			
NXT	Samoa Joe			

WWE BASIC SERIES 75 (2017)		MOC	LOOSE	VALUE
RAW	Braun Strowman			
RAW	Brock Lesnar			
RAW	Chris Jericho			
RAW	Finn Balor			
RAW	Lana			
RAW	Randy Orton			

WWE BASIC SERIES 76 (2017)		MOC	LOOSE	VALUE
SMACKDOWN	AJ Styles			
SMACKDOWN	Dolph Ziggler			
SMACKDOWN	John Cena			
LEGENDS	"Macho King" Randy Savage			
RAW	Sami Zayn			
SMACKDOWN	The Rock			

WWE BASIC SERIES 77 (2017)		MOC	LOOSE	VALUE
RAW	Corey Graves			
RAW	Dean Ambrose			
RAW	Finn Balor			
RAW	Roman Reigns			
RAW	Seth Rollins			

WWE BASIC SERIES 78 (2018)	CHASE	MOC	LOOSE	VALUE
AJ Styles				
Braun Strowman				
Kevin Owens				
Natalya				
Shane McMahon				
The Rock				

WWE BASIC SERIES 79 (2018)	CHASE	MOC	LOOSE	VALUE
Baron Corbin				
Neville				
Nia Jax				
Samoa Joe				
Stone Cold Steve Austin				
TJP				

WWE BASIC SERIES 80 (2018)	CHASE	MOC	LOOSE	VALUE
Brock Lesnar				
Chris Jericho				
Rich Swann				
Roman Reigns				
Sasha Banks				

WWE BASIC SERIES 81 (2018)	CHASE	MOC	LOOSE	VALUE
Dana Brooke				
Kofi Kingston				
Rhyno				
Sami Zayn				
Seth Rollins				

WWE BASIC SERIES 82 (2018)	CHASE	MOC	LOOSE	VALUE
AJ Styles				
Becky Lynch				
John Cena				
Luke Harper				
Shinsuke Nakamura				

WWE BASIC SERIES 83 (2018)	CHASE	MOC	LOOSE	VALUE
Alicia Fox				
Kurt Angle				
Randy Orton				
Triple H				
Tye Dillinger				

WWE BASIC SERIES 84 (2018)	CHASE	MOC	LOOSE	VALUE
Dean Ambrose				
Finn Balor				
Kevin Owens				
Naomi				
Rusev				

WWE BASIC SERIES 85 (2018)	CHASE	MOC	LOOSE	VALUE
AJ Styles				
Alexa Bliss				
Bobby Roode				
John Cena				
Seth Rollins				

WWE BASIC SERIES 86 (2018)	MOC	LOOSE	VALUE
Akira Tozawa			
Charlotte Flair			
Dolph Ziggler			
Roman Reigns			
The Rock			

WWE BASIC SERIES 87 (2018)	MOC	LOOSE	VALUE
AJ Styles			
Bayley			
Dean Ambrose			
Jason Jordan			
The Miz			

WWE BASIC SERIES 88 (2018)	MOC	LOOSE	VALUE
Baron Corbin			
Chad Gable			
Elias			
John Cena			
Sasha Banks			

WWE BASIC SERIES 89 (2018)	MOC	LOOSE	VALUE
Carmella			
Cesaro			
Kalisto			
Kurt Angle			
Sheamus			

WWE BASIC SERIES 90 (2019)		MOC	LOOSE	VALUE
	Aiden English			
	Kane			
	Roman Reigns (Superman Punch Shirt)			
CHASE	Roman Reigns (Shield Shirt)			
	Ronda Rousey			
	The Miz			

WWE BASIC SERIES 91 (2019)		MOC	LOOSE	VALUE
	Alexa Bliss			
	Dean Ambrose (Blank Shirt)			
CHASE	Dean Ambrose (Shield Shirt)			
	Drew Gulak			
	Finn Balor			
	Shinsuke Nakamura			

WWE BASIC SERIES 92 (2019)		MOC	LOOSE	VALUE
	Jeff Hardy			
	John Cena			
	Mandy Rose			
	Samoa Joe			
	Seth Rollins (Kingslayer Shirt)			
CHASE	Seth Rollins (Shield Shirt)			

WWE BASIC SERIES 93 (2019)		MOC	LOOSE	VALUE
	Bayley			
	Jinder Mahal			
	"Macho Man" Randy Savage (Yellow Lightning Bolts)			
CHASE	"Macho Man" Randy Savage (White Lightning Bolts)			
	Triple H			
	The Undertaker			

WWE BASIC SERIES 94 (2019)		MOC	LOOSE	VALUE
	Big E			
	Kofi Kingston			
	Randy Orton			
	"Woken" Matt Hardy (Delete Shirt)			
CHASE	"Woken" Matt Hardy (Mower Of Lawn Shirt)			
	Xavier Woods			

WWE BASIC SERIES 95 (2019)		MOC	LOOSE	VALUE
	AJ Styles			
	Bray Wyatt			
	Kurt Angle			
	Rusev			
	Sonya Deville (Red Gear)			
CHASE	Sonya Deville (Black Gear)			

	WWE BASIC SERIES 96 (2019)	MOC	LOOSE	VALUE
	Bobby Roode			
	Daniel Bryan			
	Kevin Owens			
	Sami Zayn (Patch Gear)			
CHASE	Sami Zayn (Black & Red Gear)			
	Sasha Banks			

	WWE BASIC SERIES 97 - SUMMERSLAM (2019)	MOC	LOOSE	VALUE
	AJ Styles			
	Bret "Hitman" Hart			
	Jeff Hardy			
	Razor Ramon			
	The Miz (White Trunks)			
CHASE	The Miz (Black Trunks)			

	WWE BASIC SERIES 98 (2019)	MOC	LOOSE	VALUE
	Elias			
	Finn Balor			
	Ruby Riott			
	Tony Nese (White Trunks)			
CHASE	Tony Nese (Silver Trunks)			
	Ultimate Warrior			

WWE BASIC SERIES 99 (2019)		MOC	LOOSE	VALUE
	Ariya Daivari (White Trunks)			
CHASE	Ariya Daivari (Black Trunks)			
	Becky Lynch			
	Drew McIntyre			
	Rey Mysterio			
	Shinsuke Nakamura			

WWE BASIC SERIES 100 (2019)		MOC	LOOSE	VALUE
	John Cena			
	Shawn Michaels (Red Tights)			
CHASE	Shawn Michaels (White Tights w/ Red)			
	The Rock			
	Stone Cold Steve Austin			
	The Undertaker			

WWE BASIC SERIES 101 (2019)		MOC	LOOSE	VALUE
	AJ Styles			
	Ali (Grey & Purple)			
CHASE	Ali (Green & Black)			
	Bobby Lashley			
	Ronda Rousey			
	Sarah Logan			

WWE BASIC SERIES 102 (2020)		MOC	LOOSE	VALUE
	Constable Baron Corbin			
	Drake Maverick (Green)			
CHASE	Drake Maverick (Black)			
	Jeff Hardy			
	Seth Rollins			
	The Miz			

WWE BASIC SERIES 103 (2020)		MOC	LOOSE	VALUE
	AJ Styles			
	Becky Lynch (The Man Shirt)			
CHASE	Becky Lynch (Relent-Lass Shirt)			
	Brock Lesnar			
	Kofi Kingston			
	Matt Riddle			

WWE BASIC SERIES 104 (2020)		MOC	LOOSE	VALUE
	Alexa Bliss			
	Daniel Bryan			
	Keith Lee (Blue)			
CHASE	Keith Lee (Black)			
	Randy Orton			
	Rey Mysterio			

WWE BASIC SERIES 105 (2020)		MOC	LOOSE	VALUE
	John Cena			
	Lars Sullivan			
	Paige			
	Roman Reigns			
	Ronda Rousey (White Top)			
CHASE	Ronda Rousey (Black Top)			

WWE BASIC SERIES 106 (2020)		MOC	LOOSE	VALUE
	Carmella (Blue)			
CHASE	Carmella (Red)			
	Finn Balor			
	Johnny Gargano			
	R-Truth			
	Triple H			

WWE BASIC SERIES 107 (2020)		MOC	LOOSE	VALUE
	Bianca Belair			
	Braun Strowman			
	EC3			
	Shinsuke Nakamura (Black & Red)			
CHASE	Shinsuke Nakamura (Blue & Black)			
	The Rock			

		WWE BASIC SERIES 108 (2020)	MOC	LOOSE	VALUE
		AJ Styles (Black & Red)			
CHASE		AJ Styles (Black & Gold)			
		Aleister Black			
		Angelo Dawkins			
		Montez Ford			
		Roman Reigns			

		WWE BASIC SERIES 109 - SUMMERSLAM (2020)	MOC	LOOSE	VALUE
		Becky Lynch			
		Lana (Blue)			
CHASE		Lana (Red)			
		Ricochet			
		Seth Rollins			
		The Undertaker			

		WWE BASIC SERIES 110 (2020)	MOC	LOOSE	VALUE
		Finn Balor			
		John Cena			
		Kofi Kingston			
		Liv Morgan			
		Mike Kanellis (Rose Trunks)			
CHASE		Mike Kanellis (Kanellis Trunks)			

WWE BASIC SERIES 111 (2020)		MOC	LOOSE	VALUE
	Bray Wyatt			
	Erick Rowan			
	Jeff Hardy			
	Kevin Owens			
	Nikki Cross (Blue & Pink Shirt)			
CHASE	Nikki Cross (Black & Blue Shirt)			

WWE BASIC SERIES 112 (2020)		MOC	LOOSE	VALUE
	Adam Cole			
	Bobby Lashley (Tights)			
CHASE	Bobby Lashley (Trunks)			
	Braun Strowman			
	Sasha Banks			
	Seth Rollins			

WWE BASIC SERIES 113 (2020)		MOC	LOOSE	VALUE
	Buddy Murphy			
	Drew McIntyre			
	Edge (Purple Boots)			
CHASE	Edge (Silver Boots)			
	John Cena			
	Mia Yim			

WWE BASIC SERIES 114 (2021)		MOC	LOOSE	VALUE
	Kofi Kingston			
	Rhea Ripley			
	Ricochet (Green & Black Shorts)			
CHASE	Ricochet (Yellow & Black Shorts)			
	Shorty G			
	"The Fiend" Bray Wyatt			

WWE BASIC SERIES 115 (2021)		MOC	LOOSE	VALUE
	Becky Lynch			
	Big E			
	Braun Strowman			
	Humberto Carrillo (Black Tights)			
CHASE	Humberto Carrillo (White Tights)			
	Tegan Nox			

WWE BASIC SERIES 116 (2021)		MOC	LOOSE	VALUE
	Dakota Kai			
	Kevin Owens			
	Roderick Strong (Green Trunks)			
CHASE	Roderick Strong (Black Trunks)			
	Seth Rollins			
	Sheamus			

WWE BASIC SERIES 117 (2021)		MOC	LOOSE	VALUE
	Otis			
	Roman Reigns			
	Toni Storm (Blue)			
CHASE	Toni Storm (Red)			
	Tucker			
	The Undertaker			

WWE BASIC SERIES 118 (2021)		MOC	LOOSE	VALUE
	Austin Theory (Black Tights)			
CHASE	Austin Theory (Red Tights)			
	Erik			
	Finn Balor			
	Ivar			
	Jeff Hardy			

WWE BASIC SERIES 119 (2021)		MOC	LOOSE	VALUE
	Dominik Dijakovic			
	John Cena			
	Lacey Evans (Black & Red)			
CHASE	Lacey Evans (Blue & Yellow)			
	Randy Orton			
	Triple H			

WWE BASIC SERIES 120 (2021)		MOC	LOOSE	VALUE
	Edge			
	Karrion Kross			
	Pete Dunne			
	Scarlett (Bodysuit)			
CHASE	Scarlett (2-Piece)			
	Shawn Michaels			

WWE BASIC SERIES 121 - SUMMERSLAM (2021)		MOC	LOOSE	VALUE
	Apollo Crews (Grey & Black Trunks)			
CHASE	Apollo Crews (Black & Blue Trunks)			
	Bayley			
	Kane			
	Rey Mysterio			
	Roman Reigns			

WWE BASIC SERIES 122 (2021)		MOC	LOOSE	VALUE
	Charlotte Flair			
	Chelsea Green (Purple)			
CHASE	Chelsea Green (Black)			
	Damian Priest			
	Drew McIntyre			

WWE BASIC SERIES 123 (2021)		MOC	LOOSE	VALUE
	Braun Strowman			
	Bobby Lashley			
	Dexter Lumis			
	Jake Atlas (Black Shorts)			
CHASE	Jake Atlas (White Shorts)			
	Otis			

WWE BASIC SERIES 124 (2021)		MOC	LOOSE	VALUE
	Angel Garza (Yellow)			
CHASE	Angel Garza (Green)			
	Io Shirai			
	Kyle O'Reilly			
	Rey Mysterio			
	Seth Rollins			

WWE BASIC SERIES 125 (2022)		MOC	LOOSE	VALUE
	Elias			
	Ember Moon			
	Isaiah "Swerve" Scott (Green)			
CHASE	Isaiah "Swerve" Scott (Red)			
	Jeff Hardy			
	The Rock			

WWE BASIC SERIES 126 (2022)		MOC	LOOSE	VALUE
	Bobby Fish			
	Drew McIntyre			
	"Macho Man" Randy Savage			
	Mandy Rose (Blue)			
CHASE	Mandy Rose (Pink)			
	Seth Rollins			

WWE BASIC SERIES 127 (2022)		MOC	LOOSE	VALUE
	Joaquinn Wilde (Face Paint)			
CHASE	Joaquinn Wilde (Unpainted)			
	Keith Lee			
	Rey Mysterio			
	Santos Escobar			
	Shayna Baszler			

WWE BASIC SERIES 128 (2022)		MOC	LOOSE	VALUE
	Big E			
	Edge			
	MVP			
	Raul Mendoza (Face Paint)			
CHASE	Raul Mendoza (Unpainted)			
	Sasha Banks			

	WWE BASIC SERIES 129 (2022)	MOC	LOOSE	VALUE
	Carmella			
	Dominik Mysterio			
	Noam Dar			
	The Miz			
	Roman Reigns (Black Shirt)			
CHASE	Roman Reigns (White Shirt)			

	WWE BASIC SERIES 130 (2022)	MOC	LOOSE	VALUE
	AJ Styles			
	Gran Metalik			
	John Cena			
	Johnny Gargano (The Way Gear)			
CHASE	Johnny Gargano (HBK Gear)			
	Omos			

	WWE BASIC SERIES 131 (2022)	MOC	LOOSE	VALUE
	Bianca Bel Air			
	Candice LaRae (The Way Gear)			
CHASE	Candice LaRae (1-2-3 Kid Gear)			
	Happy Corbin			
	Lince Dorado			
	Randy Orton			

WWE BASIC SERIES 132 (2022)		MOC	LOOSE	VALUE
	Bobby Lashley			
	Kushida			
	Rey Mysterio			
	Riddle			
	Tamina (Blue)			
CHASE	Tamina (Green)			

WWE BASIC SERIES 133 (2022)		MOC	LOOSE	VALUE
	Cedric Alexander (Red)			
CHASE	Cedric Alexander (Black)			
	Finn Balor			
	Natalya			
	Roman Reigns			
	Stone Cold Steve Austin			

WWE BASIC SERIES 134 (2022)		MOC	LOOSE	VALUE
	Becky Lynch			
	Indi Hartwell			
	Sami Zayn			
	Seth Rollins			
	Shelton Benjamin (Gold)			
CHASE	Shelton Benjamin (Black & Bronze)			

WWE BASIC SERIES 135 (2023)		MOC	LOOSE	VALUE
	Brock Lesnar			
	Bron Breakker			
	Damian Priest			
	Nikki A.S.H.			
	Reggie (Red Pants)			
CHASE	Reggie (White Pants)			

WWE BASIC SERIES 136 (2023)		MOC	LOOSE	VALUE
	Bobby Roode			
	Cody Rhodes			
	Dolph Ziggler (Pink)			
CHASE	Dolph Ziggler (Blue)			
	Goldberg			
	Xia Li			

WWE BASIC SERIES 137 (2023)		MOC	LOOSE	VALUE
	Aliyah			
	Austin Theory			
	Commander Azeez			
	Roman Reigns			
	Seth Rollins (White Kneepad On Right Knee)			
CHASE	Seth Rollins (White Kneepad On Left Knee)			

WWE BASIC SERIES 138 (2023)		MOC	LOOSE	VALUE
	Drew McIntyre			
	Edge			
	Gigi Dolin			
	Jacy Jayne			
	Shinsuke Nakamura (Black & White Pants)			
CHASE	Shinsuke Nakamura (White & Red Pants)			

WWE BASIC SERIES 139 (2023)		MOC	LOOSE	VALUE
	Hulk Hogan			
	John Cena			
	Liv Morgan			
	Pat McAfee (Plain Black Shirt)			
CHASE	Pat McAfee (For The Brand Shirt)			
	Riddle			

WWE BASIC SERIES 140 (2023)		MOC	LOOSE	VALUE
	Ciampa (Tights)			
CHASE	Ciampa (Trunks)			
	Cody Rhodes			
	Randy Orton			
	Rey Mysterio			
	Ronda Rousey			

WWE BASIC SERIES 141 (2023)		MOC	LOOSE	VALUE
	Bianca Belair			
	Brock Lesnar			
	LA Knight (Red Trunks)			
CHASE	LA Knight (Yellow Trunks)			
	Seth Rollins			
	The Rock			

WWE BASIC SERIES 142 (2023)		MOC	LOOSE	VALUE
	Charlotte Flair			
	Honky Tonk Man (Red Tights)			
CHASE	Honky Tonk Man (Blue Tights)			
	Hulk Hogan			
	Top Dolla			
	The Undertaker			

WWE BASIC SERIES 143 (2023)		MOC	LOOSE	VALUE
	Ashante "Thee" Adonis			
	Becky Lynch			
	Cody Rhodes			
	John Cena			
	Mr. T (Short Sleeves)			
CHASE	Mr. T (Long Sleeves)			

WWE BASIC SERIES 144 (2024)		MOC	LOOSE	VALUE
	B-Fab			
	Dominik Mysterio			
	Karrion Kross			
	Rey Mysterio			
	Ultimate Warrior (Orange Trunks)			
CHASE	Ultimate Warrior (Yellow Trunks)			

WWE BASIC SERIES 145 (2024)		MOC	LOOSE	VALUE
	Gunther			
	Kane			
	Ludwig Kaiser (Blue Trunks)			
CHASE	Ludwig Kaiser (Red Trunks)			
	Sami Zayn			
	Tiffany Stratton			

WWE BASIC SERIES 146 (2024)		MOC	LOOSE	VALUE
	Bret "Hit Man" Hart (Pink Singlet)			
CHASE	Bret "Hit Man" Hart (Pink & Black Singlet)			
	Giovanni Vinci			
	Kevin Owens			
	Roman Reigns			
	Shayna Baszler			

	MAIN EVENT SERIES 147 (2024)	MOC	LOOSE	VALUE
	AJ Styles			
	Brock Lesnar			
	Katana Chance			
	"Million Dollar Man" Ted Dibiase (Black Suit)			
CHASE	"Million Dollar Man" Ted Dibiase (Green Suit)			
	Seth Rollins			

	MAIN EVENT SERIES 148 (2024)	MOC	LOOSE	VALUE
	Carmello Hayes			
	Hulk Hogan			
	John Cena (Transluscent)			
CHASE	John Cena (Green Shirt)			
	Kayden Carter			
	"Rowdy" Roddy Piper			

	MAIN EVENT SERIES 149 (2024)	MOC	LOOSE	VALUE
	Cody Rhodes			
	Eddie Guerrero (Black Tights)			
CHASE	Eddie Guerrero (Green Tights)			
	Maxxine Dupri			
	The Miz			
	Sheamus			

MAIN EVENT SERIES 150 (2024)		MOC	LOOSE	VALUE
	CM Punk (Blue Stars)			
CHASE	CM Punk (Red Stars)			
	Lita			
	Rey Mysterio			
	Stone Cold Steve Austin			
	The Rock			

MAIN EVENT SERIES 151 (2025)		MOC	LOOSE	VALUE
	Andre Chase			
	Rob Van Dam			
	Roman Reigns			
	Solo Sikoa			
	Thea Hail (Black Gear)			
CHASE	Thea Hail (Chase U Gear)			

MAIN EVENT SERIES 152 (2025)		MOC	LOOSE	VALUE
	Batista			
	Liv Morgan			
	Ricky Steamboat (Red Tights)			
CHASE	Ricky Steamboat (White Trunks)			
	Seth Freakin' Rollins			
	Stone Cold Steve Austin			

MAIN EVENT SERIES 153 (2025)		MOC	LOOSE	VALUE
	Cody Rhodes			
	Duke Hudson			
	Jey Uso			
	Mr. Perfect (Blue Singlet)			
CHASE	Mr. Perfect (Black Singlet)			
	Rhea Ripley			

MAIN EVENT SERIES 154 (2025)		MOC	LOOSE	VALUE
	AJ Styles			
	CM Punk			
	Jake "The Snake" Roberts			
	Kiana James (Blue)			
CHASE	Kiana James (Green)			
	Randy Orton			

MAIN EVENT SERIES 155 (2025)		MOC	LOOSE	VALUE
	Andrade			
	Jimmy Uso			
	LA Knight			
	Lyra Valkyria (Black, Red & Gold)			
CHASE	Lyra Valkyria (Black, Green & Gold)			
	Sid Justice			

MAIN EVENT SERIES 156 (2025)		MOC	LOOSE	VALUE
	Chelsea Green (Ghostbusters Gear)			
CHASE	Chelsea Green (Black & Gold)			
	Finn Balor			
	Joaquin Wilde			
	The Rock			
	Triple H			

MAIN EVENT SERIES 157 (2025)		MOC	LOOSE	VALUE
	Alundra Blayze			
	Drew McIntyre			
	Jey Uso			
	Nathan Frazer (Purple Tights)			
CHASE	Nathan Frazer (Red Tights)			
	Rey Mysterio			

MAIN EVENT SERIES 158 (2025)		MOC	LOOSE	VALUE
	Damian Priest			
	Kofi Kingston			
	Oba Femi			
	Roman Reigns			
	Trick Williams (Grey Shorts)			
CHASE	Trick Williams (Red Shorts)			

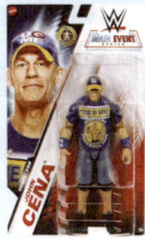

MAIN EVENT SERIES 159 (2025)		MOC	LOOSE	VALUE
	Cody Rhodes			
	John Cena			
	Tiffany Stratton			
	Wendy Choo (Black Onesie)			
CHASE	Wendy Choo (Blue Onesie)			
	Xavier Woods			

MAIN EVENT SERIES 160 (2025)		MOC	LOOSE	VALUE
	"Dirty" Dominik Mysterio			
	Gunther			
	Kelani Jordan			
	Roman Reigns			
	Tonga Loa			
CHASE				

MAIN EVENT SERIES 161 (2026)		MOC	LOOSE	VALUE
	Brutus "The Barber" Beefcake			
	Jade Cargill			
	Jey Uso			
	Jimmy Uso			
	The Undertaker			
CHASE				

2010 ROYAL RUMBLE	1 OF 1,000	MOC	LOOSE	VALUE
Beth Phoenix				
Chris Jericho				
CM Punk				
Cody Rhodes				
Edge				
Triple H				

2010 ROYAL RUMBLE HERITAGE SERIES	1 OF 1,000	MOC	LOOSE	VALUE
Christian				
John Cena				
Randy Orton				
Rey Mysterio				
Sheamus				
The Undertaker				

2010 ELIMINATION CHAMBER	1 OF 1,000	MOC	LOOSE	VALUE
Batista				
Chris Jericho				
Drew McIntyre				
John Cena				
Rey Mysterio				
The Undertaker				

2010 WRESTLEMANIA HERITAGE SERIES	1 OF 1,000	MOC	LOOSE	VALUE
Batista				
Edge				
John Cena				
Randy Orton				
Stone Cold Steve Austin				
The Undertaker				

2010 WRESTLEMANIA XXVI (TOYS 'R' US)	MOC	LOOSE	VALUE
Chris Jericho			
Christian			
Drew Mcintyre			
Kane			
Matt Hardy			
Shawn Michaels			
Shelton Benjamin			

2010 OVER THE LIMIT	MOC	LOOSE	VALUE
Big Show			
CM Punk			
Jack Swagger			
John Cena			
Rey Mysterio			
R-Truth			

2010 SURVIVOR SERIES	1 OF 1,000	MOC	LOOSE	VALUE
John Cena				
John Morrison				
Kofi Kingston				
Rey Mysterio				
The Miz				
The Undertaker				

2011 WRESTLEMANIA HERITAGE SERIES	1 OF 1,000	MOC	LOOSE	VALUE
CM Punk				
John Cena				
Kane				
Melina				
Randy Orton				
Triple H				

2011 WRESTLEMANIA XXVII		MOC	LOOSE	VALUE
Alberto Del Rio				
Christian				
John Cena				
John Morrison				
Randy Orton				
Triple H				

2011 EXTREME RULES	1 OF 1,000	MOC	LOOSE	VALUE
Alberto Del Rio				
Christian				
John Cena				
Rey Mysterio				
R-Truth				
Sheamus				

2011 SUMMERSLAM	1 OF 1,000	MOC	LOOSE	VALUE
Edge				
John Cena				
Randy Orton				
Rey Mysterio				
The Great Khali				
Triple H				

2011 SURVIVOR SERIES	1 OF 1,000	MOC	LOOSE	VALUE
Big Show				
Chris Masters				
Evan Bourne				
John Cena				
Sheamus				
The Rock				

2011 TLC: TABLES, LADDERS & CHAIRS	1 OF 1,000	MOC	LOOSE	VALUE
Edge				
John Cena				
John Morrison				
Rey Mysterio				
Sheamus				
Wade Barrett				

BEST OF PAY-PER-VIEW: 2011 (TOYS 'R' US)		MOC	LOOSE	VALUE
CAPITAL PUNISHMENT	Christian			
OVER THE LIMIT	John Cena			
MONEY IN THE BANK	Mark Henry			
ROYAL RUMBLE	Rey Mysterio			

2012 WRESTLEMANIA XXVIII (TOYS 'R' US)	MOC	LOOSE	VALUE
John Cena			
Sheamus			
The Rock			
Triple H			

TRIBUTE TO THE TROOPS 2012 (K-MART)	MOC	LOOSE	VALUE
Big Show			
Rey Mysterio			
Randy Orton (Brown Vest)			
Randy Orton (Green Vest)			
John Cena			

BEST OF PAY-PER-VIEW: 2012 (TOYS 'R' US)		MOC	LOOSE	VALUE
MONEY IN THE BANK	Alberto Del Rio			
EXTREME RULES	Brock Lesnar			
NO WAY OUT	Dolph Ziggler			
OVER THE LIMIT	Randy Orton			
BUILD-A-FIGURE	Teddy Long			

2012 SURVIVOR SERIES (K-MART)	MOC	LOOSE	VALUE
CM Punk			
Ryback			

2012 TLC: TABLES, LADDERS & CHAIRS (TOYS 'R' US)	MOC	LOOSE	VALUE
Alberto Del Rio			
Kofi Kingston			
Mark Henry			
Sheamus			

BEST OF PAY-PER-VIEW: 2013 (TOYS 'R' US)		MOC	LOOSE	VALUE
WRESTLEMANIA 29	Alberto Del Rio			
WRESTLEMANIA 29	Sheamus			
WRESTLEMANIA 29	The Rock			
WRESTLEMANIA 29	The Undertaker			
BUILD-A-FIGURE	Booker T			

2014 WRESTLEMANIA XXX	MOC	LOOSE	VALUE
Brock Lesnar			
John Cena			
The Rock			
The Undertaker			

2014 SUMMERSLAM	MOC	LOOSE	VALUE
CM Punk			
Rey Mysterio			
Shawn Michaels			
Ted Dibiase			
Triple H			
The Undertaker			

BEST OF PAY-PER-VIEW: 2014 (TOYS 'R' US)		MOC	LOOSE	VALUE
MONEY IN THE BANK	Damien Sandow			
EXTREME RULES	Daniel Bryan			
PAYBACK	Dolph Ziggler			
ROYAL RUMBLE	Kofi Kingston			
BUILD-A-FIGURE	Paul Bearer			

2015 WRESTLEMANIA HERITAGE SERIES	MOC	LOOSE	VALUE
Hulk Hogan			
John Cena			
Shawn Michaels			
The Rock			

2016 WRESTLEMANIA 32		MOC	LOOSE	VALUE
Cesaro				
Eddie Guerrero				
Razor Ramon				
Roman Reigns				

2016 SUMMERSLAM			MOC	LOOSE	VALUE
2005	Batista				
1992	British Bulldog				
1989	"Hacksaw" Jim Duggan				
1998	The Undertaker				

2017 WRESTLEMANIA 33		MOC	LOOSE	VALUE
Chris Jericho				
Roman Reigns				
Stone Cold Steve Austin				
The Undertaker				

2017 SUMMERSLAM		MOC	LOOSE	VALUE
Dusty Rhodes				
Nikki Bella				
Seth Rollins				
The Rock				

2018 WRESTLEMANIA 34	MOC	LOOSE	VALUE
AJ Styles			
Bayley			
Big Show			
Dean Ambrose			
Mojo Rawley			
Seth Rollins			

WWE 2018 SUMMERSLAM BASICS	MOC	LOOSE	VALUE
John Cena			
Kurt Angle			
Ric Flair			
Roman Reigns			
Shane McMahon			
Shinsuke Nakamura			

2019 WRESTLEMANIA 35	MOC	LOOSE	VALUE
Charlotte Flair			
Elias			
John Cena			
Kevin Nash			
Trish Stratus			
"Woken" Matt Hardy			

2020 WRESTLEMANIA 36	MOC	LOOSE	VALUE
Batista			
Becky Lynch			
Seth Rollins			
Shane McMahon			
Stephanie McMahon			
The Rock			

2021 WRESTLEMANIA 37	MOC	LOOSE	VALUE
Andrade			
Drew McIntyre			
"The Fiend" Bray Wyatt			
Ricochet			
Andre The Giant (w/ Ring Cart)			
"Macho Man" Randy Savage (w/ Ring Cart)			

2022 WRESTLEMANIA 38	MOC	LOOSE	VALUE
Bianca Belair			
Hulk Hogan			
Seth Rollins			
Sheamus			

2023 WRESTLEMANIA 39	MOC	LOOSE	VALUE
Andre The Giant			
Bianca Belair			
Kane			
The Undertaker			

2024 WRESTLEMANIA 40	MOC	LOOSE	VALUE
Batista			
Muhammad Ali		CANCELED	
Roman Reigns			
Seth Rollins			

SIGNATURE SERIES 0 (2010)	MOC	LOOSE	VALUE
Batista			
Chris Jericho			
John Cena			
Shawn Michaels			

SIGNATURE SERIES 1 (2011)		MOC	LOOSE	VALUE
BLACK	Edge			
WHITE	Edge			
	John Cena			
	Randy Orton			
	Rey Mysterio			
	Triple H			
	The Undertaker			

SIGNATURE SERIES 2 (2012)	MOC	LOOSE	VALUE
Big Show			
John Cena			
Kane			
Randy Orton			
Rey Mysterio			
The Miz			

WWE SIGNATURE SERIES 3 (2012)	MOC	LOOSE	VALUE
John Cena			
Rey Mysterio			
The Rock			

SIGNATURE SERIES 4 (2012)		MOC	LOOSE	VALUE
JORTS	John Cena			
CAMO	John Cena			
	Rey Mysterio			
	Sheamus			

SIGNATURE SERIES 5 (2013)	MOC	LOOSE	VALUE
CM Punk			
John Cena			
Kane			
Rey Mysterio			
Sin Cara			
The Rock			

SIGNATURE SERIES 6 (2014)	MOC	LOOSE	VALUE
Alberto Del Rio			
Big Show			
CM Punk			
John Cena			
Kane			
Rey Mysterio			
R-Truth			
Sin Cara			
Stone Cold Steve Austin			

SIGNATURE SERIES 7 (2015)	MOC	LOOSE	VALUE
Batista			
Bray Wyatt			
Daniel Bryan			
Dean Ambrose			
Hulk Hogan			
John Cena			
Stone Cold Steve Austin			

BEST OF 2010	CHASE	MOC	LOOSE	VALUE
Batista				
Evan Bourne				
Hornswoggle				
John Cena				
Mark Henry				
Rey Mysterio				

BEST OF 2011	MOC	LOOSE	VALUE
Big Show			
John Cena			
Kofi Kingston			
Randy Orton			
Rey Mysterio			
Santino Marella			

BEST OF 2012	MOC	LOOSE	VALUE
Alberto Del Rio			
Brodus Clay			
Daniel Bryan			
Rey Mysterio			
Sin Cara			
The Great Khali			

BEST OF 2013	MOC	LOOSE	VALUE
Brock Lesnar			
Kaitlyn			
Randy Orton			
Rey Mysterio			
Tensai			
The Undertaker			

BEST OF 2014		MOC	LOOSE	VALUE
Cesaro				
El Torito				
John Cena				
Roman Reigns				
Sin Cara				
The Undertaker				

TOP PICKS 2018		MOC	LOOSE	VALUE
AJ Styles				
John Cena				
Roman Reigns				
Seth Rollins				

TOP PICKS 2019			MOC	LOOSE	VALUE
	AJ Styles				
	Jeff Hardy				
	John Cena				
	Seth Rollins (Black & Gold Tights)				
CHASE	Seth Rollins (Red & Black Tights)				

TOP PICKS 2020			MOC	LOOSE	VALUE
	AJ Styles				
WAVE 1	Braun Strowman				
	Finn Balor				
	John Cena				
	John Cena				
WAVE 2	Kofi Kingston				
	Roman Reigns				
	The Rock				

TOP PICKS 2021			MOC	LOOSE	VALUE
WAVE 1	Braun Strowman				
	John Cena				
	Roman Reigns				
	The Rock				
WAVE 2	Drew McIntyre				
	"The Fiend" Bray Wyatt				
	John Cena				
	The Rock				

TOP PICKS 2022			MOC	LOOSE	VALUE
WAVE 1	Big E				
	Drew McIntyre				
	John Cena				
WAVE 2	Bray Wyatt				
	Roman Reigns				
	The Undertaker				
WAVE 3	Brock Lesnar				
	Seth Rollins				
	The Rock				
WAVE 4	John Cena				
	Randy Orton				
	Rey Mysterio				

TOP PICKS 2023			MOC	LOOSE	VALUE
WAVE 1	Big E				
	Drew McIntyre				
	John Cena				
WAVE 2	AJ Styles				
	Brock Lesnar				
	The Rock				
WAVE 3	Cody Rhodes				
	Riddle				
	Roman Reigns				

TOP PICKS 2024		MOC	LOOSE	VALUE
WAVE 1	Cody Rhodes			
	Drew McIntyre			
	Randy Orton			
WAVE 2	The Rock			
	Seth Rollins			
	The Undertaker			
WAVE 3	Cody Rhodes			
	John Cena			
	Roman Reigns			
WAVE 4	Dominik Mysterio			
	LA Knight			
	Seth Rollins			

TOP PICKS 2025		MOC	LOOSE	VALUE
WAVE 1	LA Knight			
	The Rock			
	Seth Freakin' Rollins			
WAVE 2	AJ Styles			
	Cody Rhodes			
	Drew McIntyre			
WAVE 3	CM Punk			
	Roman Reigns			
	The Undertaker			
WAVE 4	Jey Uso			
	John Cena			
	Randy Orton			

BEST OF MAIN EVENT SERIES 1	MOC	LOOSE	VALUE
Cody Rhodes			
Gunther			
John Cena			
Roman Reigns			

WWE RAW ON NETFLIX	MOC	LOOSE	VALUE
CM Punk			
Dominik Mysterio			
Drew McIntyre			
Gunther			
Jey Uso			
John Cena			
Liv Morgan			
Rey Mysterio			
Sami Zayn			
Seth Freakin' Rollins			
Sheamus			

ENTRANCE GREATS (2010)		MIB	LOOSE	VALUE
SERIES 1	Rey Mysterio			
	Shawn Michaels			
	Triple H			
SERIES 2	"Million Dollar Man" Ted Dibiase			
	Chris Jericho			
	"Rowdy" Roddy Piper			
SERIES 3	The Rock			
	The Undertaker			

SUPERSTAR MATCH-UPS (2010)		MIB	LOOSE	VALUE
SERIES 1	John Cena			
	Rey Mysterio (Black & Orange)			
	Rey Mysterio (Black & Green)			
	Rey Mysterio (Blue & Yellow)			
	Shawn Michaels			
	Triple H			
SERIES 2 (K-MART)	Rey Mysterio (Blue & Black)			
	Rey Mysterio (Blue & White)			
	Sin Cara			

ULTIMATE FAN PACKS		MOC	LOOSE	VALUE
SERIES 1	Finn Balor			
	John Cena			
	"Macho" Man Randy Savage			
	Roman Reigns			
SERIES 2	AJ Styles			
	Enzo Amore			
	Jeff Hardy			

MAIN EVENT ROLE PLAY SERIES (2025)	MOC	LOOSE	VALUE
Rey Mysterio (w/ Mask)			
Roman Reigns (w/ Gauntlets)			

RINGSIDE BATTLE SERIES 1 (2023)	MOC	LOOSE	VALUE
Rey Mysterio			
The Rock			

ZOMBIES SERIES 1 (2016)	MOC	LOOSE	VALUE
Bray Wyatt			
Dean Ambrose			
John Cena			
Paige			
Roman Reigns			
The Rock			
Triple H			
The Undertaker			

ZOMBIES SERIES 2 (2017)	MOC	LOOSE	VALUE
AJ Styles			
Brock Lesnar			
Kevin Owens			
Sasha Banks			
Seth Rollins			
Stone Cold Steve Austin			

ZOMBIES SERIES 3 (2018)	MOC	LOOSE	VALUE
Charlotte Flair			
Finn Balor			
Jeff Hardy			
Kane			
Matt Hardy			
Shinsuke Nakamura			

MUTANTS (2016)	MOC	LOOSE	VALUE
Bray Wyatt			
Brock Lesnar			
Finn Balor			
John Cena			
Stardust			
Sting			

MONSTERS (2018)	MOC	LOOSE	VALUE
Asuka (As The Phantom)			
Braun Strowman (As Frankenstein)			
Chris Jericho (As The Mummy)			
Jake "The Snake" Roberts (As The Creature)			
Roman Reigns (As The Werewolf)			
The Undertaker (As The Vampire)			

CHAMPIONS COLLECTION (K-MART)		MOC	LOOSE	VALUE
SERIES 1	Big Show			
	John Cena			
	Kane			
	Kofi Kingston			
SERIES 2	Daniel Bryan			
	The Rock			
SERIES 3	Dean Ambrose			
	John Cena			
	Randy Orton			
SERIES 4	Bad News Barrett			
	Daniel Bryan			
	Ultimate Warrior			

NXT TAKEOVER SERIES 1 (TARGET)	MOC	LOOSE	VALUE
Andrade "Cien" Almas			
Hideo Itami			
Kevin Owens			
Sami Zayn			
Samoa Joe			
Tye Dillinger			

NXT TAKEOVER SERIES 2 (TARGET)	MOC	LOOSE	VALUE
Akam			
Bobby Roode			
Eva Marie			
Johnny Gargano			
Rezar			
Tommaso Ciampa			

WWE NETWORTK SPOTLIGHT (TOYS 'R' US)	MOC	LOOSE	VALUE
Big Cass			
Brock Lesnar			
Enzo Amore			
Sting			

FAN CENTRAL SERIES 1 (K-MART)	MOC	LOOSE	VALUE
Finn Balor			
John Cena			
Ryback			
Triple H			

FAN CENTRAL SERIES 2 (TOYS 'R' US)	MOC	LOOSE	VALUE
Finn Balor			
Kevin Nash			
Randy Orton			
Rusev			

FAN CENTRAL SERIES 3 (WALMART)	MOC	LOOSE	VALUE
Bobby Roode			
Dean Ambrose			
Kevin Owens			
Ric Flair			

SUPERSTAR ENTRANCES SERIES 1 (WALMART)	MOC	LOOSE	VALUE
CM Punk			
Dolph Ziggler			
John Cena			
R-Truth			
Randy Orton			
The Miz			
Triple H			
Zack Ryder			

SUPERSTAR ENTRANCES SERIES 2 (WALMART)	MOC	LOOSE	VALUE
Daniel Bryan			
John Cena			
Ryback			
Santino Marella			
The Rock			

SUPERSTAR ENTRANCES SERIES 3 (WALMART)	MOC	LOOSE	VALUE
Brock Lesnar			
CM Punk			
Cody Rhodes			
John Cena			
"Macho Man" Randy Savage			
Sheamus			

SUPERSTAR ENTRANCES SERIES 4 (WALMART)	MOC	LOOSE	VALUE
AJ Lee			
Daniel Bryan			
Dolph Ziggler			
John Cena			
Rob Van Dam			
The Rock			

SUPERSTAR ENTRANCES SERIES 5 (WALMART)	MOC	LOOSE	VALUE
Daniel Bryan			
John Cena			
Randy Orton			
"Rowdy" Roddy Piper			
Triple H			

SUPERSTAR ENTRANCES SERIES 6 (WALMART)	MOC	LOOSE	VALUE
Bad News Barrett			
Bo Dallas			
Hulk Hogan			
John Cena			
Kofi Kingston			

THEN, NOW, FOREVER SERIES 1 (WALMART)	MOC	LOOSE	VALUE
Chris Jericho			
Seth Rollins			
Sin Cara			
The Undertaker			

THEN, NOW, FOREVER (WALMART)		MOC	LOOSE	VALUE
	Cesaro			
	Seth Rollins			
	Triple H			
	X-Pac			
BUILD-A-FIGURE	Mean Gene Okerlund			

THEN, NOW, FOREVER SERIES 2 (WALMART)	MOC	LOOSE	VALUE
Bray Wyatt			
Kevin Owens			
Seth Rollins			
Triple H			
X-Pac			

THEN, NOW, FOREVER SERIES 3 (WALMART)	MOC	LOOSE	VALUE
Neville			
Sheamus			
Stone Cold Steve Austin			
Ultimate Warrior			

BUILD-A-PAUL BEARER (WALMART)		MOC	LOOSE	VALUE
	Chris Jericho			
	Neville			
	Rusev			
	The Undertaker			
BUILD-A-FIGURE	Paul Bearer			

FLASHBACK SERIES 1 (WALMART)		MOC	LOOSE	VALUE
	"Cowboy" Bob Orton			
	"Ravishing" Rick Rude			
	Sgt. Slaughter			
	Ted Dibiase			
BUILD-A-FIGURE	Howard Finkel			

FLASHBACK SERIES 2 (WALMART)		MOC	LOOSE	VALUE
	Booker T			
	Lex Luger			
	Ric Flair			
	Sting			
BUILD-A-FIGURE	JJ Dillon			

MISCELLANEOUS WWE BASIC EXCLUSIVES		MOC	LOOSE	VALUE
RINGSIDE	AJ Styles (Red Tights)			
WALGREENS	John Cena (Black Fence T-Shirt)			
TOYS 'R' US	John Cena (Make A Wish)			
WWE 2K18	John Cena (Cena Nuff)			

WWE CHAMPIONS (2024)		MOC	LOOSE	VALUE
SERIES 1	Brock Lesnar (w/ WWE Championship)			
	Roman Reigns (w/ WWE Universal Championship)			
	The Rock (w/ Brahma Bull WWE Championship)			
SERIES 2	Hulk Hogan (w/ Winged Eagle WWE Championship)			
	John Cena (w/ Spinner WWE Championship)			
	Stone Cold Steve Austin (w/ Big Eagle WWE Championship)			
SERIES 3	Jey Uso (w/ Raw Tag Team Championship)			
	Jimmy Uso (w/ Raw Tag Team Championship)			
	The Undertaker (w/ WWE Championship)			

WWE CHAMPIONS (2025)		MOC	LOOSE	VALUE
SERIES 4	CM Punk (w/ WWE Championship)			
	Cody Rhodes (w/ Smackdown Tag Team Championship)			
	Roman Reigns (w/ Undisputed WWE Universal Championship)			
SERIES 5	Jey Uso (w/ Raw Tag Team Championship)			
	Seth Rollins (w/ WWE Championship)			
	The Rock (w/ WWE Championship)			
SERIES 6				

BATTLE PACKS & SHOWDOWNS

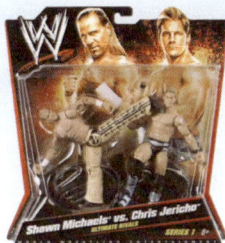

BATTLE PACKS SERIES 1 (2010)		MOC	LOOSE	VALUE
UNLIKELY ALLIES	Santino Marella			
	Beth Phoenix			
ULTIMATE RIVALS	Shawn Michaels			
	Chris Jericho			
SUPREME TEAMS	Ted Dibiase			
	Cody Rhodes			

BATTLE PACKS SERIES 2 (2010)		MOC	LOOSE	VALUE
FAMILY FURY	Carlito			
	Primo			
FAMILY FURY	Finlay			
	Hornswoggle			
SUPREME TEAMS	John Morrison			
	The Miz			

BATTLE PACKS SERIES 3 (2010)		MOC	LOOSE	VALUE
ULTIMATE RIVALS	Edge			
	Big Show			
DUAL IMPACT	Rey Mysterio			
	Evan Bourne			
SUPREME TEAMS	Shad			
	JTG			

081

BATTLE PACKS SERIES 4 (2010)		MOC	LOOSE	VALUE
ULTIMATE RIVALS	Chavo Guerrero			
	Hornswoggle			
DUAL IMPACT	Christian			
	Tommy Dreamer			
THE HART DYNASTY	DH Smith			
	Tyson Kid			

BATTLE PACKS SERIES 5 (2010)		MOC	LOOSE	VALUE
FAMILY FURY	Carlito			
	Primo			
D-GENERATION X	Triple H			
	Shawn Michaels			
ULTIMATE RIVALS	Ricky "The Dragon" Steamboat			
	Chris Jericho			

BATTLE PACKS SERIES 6 (2010)		MOC	LOOSE	VALUE
SUPREME TEAMS	Mark Henry			
	MVP			
ULTIMATE RIVALS	The Undertaker			
	Batista			
UNLIKELY ALLIES	Vladimir Kozlov			
	Ezekiel Jackson			

BATTLE PACKS SERIES 7 (2010)		MOC	LOOSE	VALUE
SUPREME TEAMS	CM Punk			
	Luke Gallows			
ULTIMATE RIVALS	Dolph Ziggler			
	John Morrison			
UNLIKELY ALLIES	The Miz			
	Big Show			

BATTLE PACKS SERIES 8 (2011)		MOC	LOOSE	VALUE
ULTIMATE RIVALS	John Cena			
	Randy Orton			
SUPREME TEAMS	Matt Hardy			
	The Great Khali			
SUPREME TEAMS	Ted Dibiase			
	Cody Rhodes			

BATTLE PACKS SERIES 9 (2011)		MOC	LOOSE	VALUE
DUAL IMPACT	Christian			
	Heath Slater			
ULTIMATE RIVALS	Sheamus			
	Triple H			
THE HART DYNASTY	Tyson Kidd			
	DH Smith			

BATTLE PACKS SERIES 10 (2011)		MOC	LOOSE	VALUE
SUPREME TEAMS	Darren Young			
	Justin Gabriel			
DUAL IMPACT	David Otunga			
	Michael Tarver			
ULTIMATE RIVALS	Randy Orton			
	Edge			

BATTLE PACKS SERIES 11 (2011)		MOC	LOOSE	VALUE
DUAL IMPACT	Drew McIntyre			
	Cody Rhodes			
FAMILY FURY	Jimmy Uso			
	Jey Uso			
FAMILY FURY	The Undertaker			
	Kane			

BATTLE PACK SERIES 12 (2012)	
Dolph Ziggler	
Kofi Kingston	
The Miz	**CANCELLED**
Daniel Bryan	
Santino Marella	
Vladimir Kozlov	

BATTLE PACK SERIES 13 (2012)	MOC	LOOSE	VALUE
John Cena			
R-Truth			
Rey Mysterio			
Cody Rhodes			
The Miz			
Alex Riley			

BATTLE PACK SERIES 14 (2012)	MOC	LOOSE	VALUE
Heath Slater			
Justin Gabriel			
"Macho Man" Randy Savage			
CM Punk			
Randy Orton			
Mason Ryan			

BATTLE PACK SERIES 15 (2012)	MOC	LOOSE	VALUE
Brie Bella			
Nikki Bella			
Sin Cara			
Daniel Bryan			
The Rock			
John Cena			

BATTLE PACK SERIES 16 (2012)	MOC	LOOSE	VALUE
Alberto Del Rio			
Big Show			
David Otunga			
Michael McGillicutty			
Randy Orton			
Christian			

BATTLE PACK SERIES 17 (2012)	MOC	LOOSE	VALUE
John Cena			
CM Punk			
Mark Henry			
Trent Barreta			
Rey Mysterio			
The Miz			

BATTLE PACK SERIES 18 (2012)	MOC	LOOSE	VALUE
CM Punk			
Triple H			
Randy Orton			
Wade Barrett			
Zack Ryder			
Dolph Ziggler			

BATTLE PACK SERIES 19 (2013)	MOC	LOOSE	VALUE
Daniel Bryan			
Big Show			
Epico			
Primo			
John Cena			
Kane			

BATTLE PACK SERIES 20 (2013)	MOC	LOOSE	VALUE
Brock Lesnar			
Triple H			
Brodus Clay			
Curt Hawkins			
Kofi Kingston			
R-Truth			

BATTLE PACK SERIES 21 (2013)	MOC	LOOSE	VALUE
Darren Young			
Titus O'Neil			
Kane			
Daniel Bryan			
Sheamus			
Randy Orton			

BATTLE PACK SERIES 22 (2013)	MOC	LOOSE	VALUE
Dolph Ziggler			
Vickie Guerrero			
Ryback			
Jinder Mahal			
Sin Cara			
Rey Mysterio			

BATTLE PACK SERIES 23 (2013)	MOC	LOOSE	VALUE
CM Punk			
Mr. McMahon			
Rey Mysterio			
Kofi Kingston			
Sin Cara			
Cody Rhodes			

BATTLE PACK SERIES 24 (2013)	MOC	LOOSE	VALUE
Naomi			
Cameron			
Seth Rollins			
Roman Reigns			
The Rock			
John Cena			

BATTLE PACK SERIES 25 (2014)	MOC	LOOSE	VALUE
Brock Lesnar			
Paul Heyman			
CM Punk			
The Undertaker			
Mark Henry			
Ryback			

BATTLE PACK SERIES 26 (2014)	MOC	LOOSE	VALUE
Nikki Bella			
Brie Bella			
Seth Rollins			
Dean Ambrose			
Triple H			
Curtis Axel			

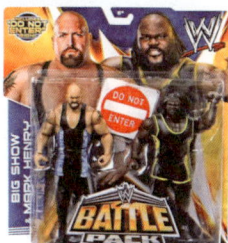

BATTLE PACK SERIES 27 (2014)	MOC	LOOSE	VALUE
Big Show			
Mark Henry			
Brodus Clay			
Tensai			
Daniel Bryan			
Randy Orton			

BATTLE PACK SERIES 28 (2014)	MOC	LOOSE	VALUE
Big E			
AJ Lee			
Jimmy Uso			
Jey Uso			
Luke Harper			
Erick Rowan			

BATTLE PACK SERIES 29 (2014)	MOC	LOOSE	VALUE
CM Punk			
Ryback			
Goldust			
Cody Rhodes			
Diego			
Fernando			

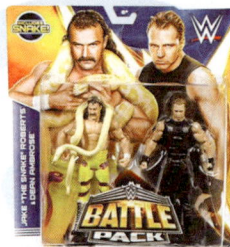

BATTLE PACK SERIES 30 (2014)	MOC	LOOSE	VALUE
Brock Lesnar			
The Undertaker			
Jake "The Snake" Roberts			
Dean Ambrose			
Xavier Woods			
R-Truth			

BATTLE PACK SERIES 31 (2015)	MOC	LOOSE	VALUE
John Cena			
Ultimate Warrior			
Luke Harper			
Erick Rowan			
Sin Cara			
Alberto Del Rio			

BATTLE PACK SERIES 32 (2015)	MOC	LOOSE	VALUE
Daniel Bryan			
Triple H			
Jimmy Uso			
Jey Uso			
Road Dogg			
Billy Gunn			

BATTLE PACK SERIES 33 (2015)	MOC	LOOSE	VALUE
Andre The Giant			
Big Show			
Rey Mysterio			
Rob Van Dam			
Shawn Michaels			
The Undertaker			

BATTLE PACK SERIES 34 (2015)	MOC	LOOSE	VALUE
Animal			
Hawk			
Hornswoggle			
El Torito			
Lana			
Rusev			

BATTLE PACK SERIES 35 (2015)	MOC	LOOSE	VALUE
Kane			
Roman Reigns			
Ryback			
Curtis Axel			
Zeb Colter			
Jack Swagger			

BATTLE PACK SERIES 36 (2015)	MOC	LOOSE	VALUE
Big E			
Kofi Kingston			
Dean Ambrose			
Seth Rollins			
Kevin Nash			
Scott Hall			

BATTLE PACK SERIES 37 (2016)		MOC	LOOSE	VALUE
SMACKDOWN	Jamie Noble			
	Joey Mercury			
RAW	Jimmy Uso			
	Jey Uso			
SMACKDOWN	Konnor			
	Viktor			

BATTLE PACK SERIES 38 (2016)		MOC	LOOSE	VALUE
SMACKDOWN	Adam Rose			
	The Bunny			
SMACKDOWN	Bray Wyatt			
	The Undertaker			
DIVAS	Nikki Bella			
	Brie Bella			

BATTLE PACK SERIES 39 (2016)		MOC	LOOSE	VALUE
SMACKDOWN	Darren Young			
	Titus O'Neil			
RAW	John Cena			
	Kevin Owens			
SMACKDOWN	Tyson Kidd			
	Cesaro			

BATTLE PACK SERIES 40 (2016)		MOC	LOOSE	VALUE
LEGENDS	Bushwhacker Luke			
	Bushwhacker Butch			
NXT	Enzo Amore			
	Big Cass			
LEGENDS	Stone Cold Steve Austin			
	Mr. McMahon			

BATTLE PACK SERIES 41 (2016)		MOC	LOOSE	VALUE
RAW	Bubba Ray Dudley			
	D-Von Dudley			
SMACKDOWN	Charlotte			
	Ric Flair			
NXT	Simon Gotch			
	Aiden English			

BATTLE PACK SERIES 42 (2016)		MOC	LOOSE	VALUE
LEGENDS	Edge			
	Christian			
SMACKDOWN	Sin Cara			
	Kalisto			
RAW	Tiple H			
	Stephanie McMahon			

BATTLE PACK SERIES 43 (2017)		MOC	LOOSE	VALUE
SMACKDOWN	Big E			
	Xavier Woods			
WOMEN'S	Nikki Bella			
	Brie Bella			
RAW	The Undertaker			
	Kane			

BATTLE PACK SERIES 43B (2017)		MOC	LOOSE	VALUE
RAW	Dean Ambrose			
	Brock Lesnar			
NXT	Finn Balor			
	Samoa Joe			
RAW	John Cena			
	Seth Rollins			
RAW	Roman Reigns			
	Sheamus			

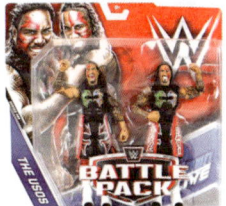

BATTLE PACK SERIES 44 (2017)		MOC	LOOSE	VALUE
NXT	Jason Jordan			
	Chad Gable			
RAW	Sami Zayn			
	Kevin Owens			
LEGENDS	Scott Hall			
	Kevin Nash			
SMACKDOWN	Jimmy Uso			
	Jey Uso			

BATTLE PACK SERIES 45 (2017)		MOC	LOOSE	VALUE
RAW	AJ Styles			
	Roman Reigns			
RAW	Enzo Amore			
	Big Cass			
NXT	Scott Dawson			
	Dash Wilder			
LEGENDS	Triple H			
	Road Dogg			

BATTLE PACK SERIES 46 (2017)		MOC	LOOSE	VALUE
SMACKDOWN	Dean Ambrose			
	Shane McMahon			
RAW	Luke Gallows			
	Karl Anderson			
SMACKDOWN	The Miz			
	Maryse			
RAW	Kofi Kingston			
	Xavier Woods			

BATTLE PACK SERIES 47 (2017)		MOC	LOOSE	VALUE
SMACKDOWN	Luke Harper			
	Bray Wyatt			
RAW	Rusev			
	Roman Reigns			
WOMEN'S	Sasha Banks			
	Charlotte Flair			
LEGENDS	Bret Hart			
	Jim "The Anvil" Neidhart			

BATTLE PACK SERIES 48 (2017)		MOC	LOOSE	VALUE
SMACKDOWN	Chad Gable			
	Jason Jordan			
SMACKDOWN	Mojo Rawley			
	Zack Ryder			
LEGENDS	Shawn Michaels			
	Diesel			

BATTLE PACK SERIES 49 (2018)	MOC	LOOSE	VALUE
Daniel Bryan			
The Miz			
Sheamus			
Cesaro			
Stephanie McMahon			
Mick Foley			

BATTLE PACK SERIES 50 (2018)	MOC	LOOSE	VALUE
Konnor			
Viktor			
Luke Gallows			
Karl Anderson			
Randy Orton			
Bray Wyatt			

BATTLE PACK SERIES 51 (2018)	MOC	LOOSE	VALUE
Dash Wilder			
Scott Dawson			
The Miz			
Maryse			
Big E			
Xavier Woods			

BATTLE PACK SERIES 52 (2018)	MOC	LOOSE	VALUE
Brock Lesnar			
Roman Reigns			
Jimmy Uso			
Jey Uso			
Sheamus			
Cesaro			
Enzo Amore (Stop Release)			
Big Cass (Stop Release)			

BATTLE PACK SERIES 53 (2018)	MOC	LOOSE	VALUE
Carmella			
James Ellsworth			
Matt Hardy			
Jeff Hardy			
Shinsuke Nakamura			
Dolph Ziggler			

BATTLE PACK SERIES 54 (2018)	MOC	LOOSE	VALUE
Braun Strowman			
Roman Reigns			
Bray Wyatt			
Finn Balor			
Nia Jax			
Alexa Bliss			
Tyler Breeze			
Fandango			

BATTLE PACK SERIES 55 (2018)	MOC	LOOSE	VALUE
Becky Lynch			
Charlotte Flair			
Big Show			
Big Cass			
Dean Ambrose			
Seth Rollins			

BATTLE PACK SERIES 56 (2019)	MOC	LOOSE	VALUE
Jason Jordan			
Kurt Angle			
Bo Dallas			
Curtis Axel			
John Cena			
Roman Reigns			

BATTLE PACK SERIES 57 (2019)	MOC	LOOSE	VALUE
Braun Strowman			
Kane			
Shinsuke Nakamura			
The Miz			
Sunil Singh			
Samir Singh			

BATTLE PACK SERIES 58 (2019)	MOC	LOOSE	VALUE
Shelton Benjamin			
Chad Gable			
Triple H			
Shawn Michaels			
Kevin Owens			
Sami Zayn			

BATTLE PACK SERIES 59 (2019)	MOC	LOOSE	VALUE
Jinder Mahal			
AJ Styles			
Jeff Hardy			
Matt Hardy			
Dean Ambrose			
Seth Rollins			

BATTLE PACK SERIES 60 (2019)	MOC	LOOSE	VALUE
Sasha Banks			
Alexa Bliss			
Goldberg			
Stone Cold Steve Austin			
Sheamus			
Cesaro			

BATTLE PACK SERIES 61 (2019)	MOC	LOOSE	VALUE
Daniel Bryan			
AJ Styles			
Billie Kay			
Peyton Royce			
Jimmy Uso			
Jey Uso			

BATTLE PACK SERIES 62 (2020)	MOC	LOOSE	VALUE
Andrade			
Zelina Vega			
Akam			
Rezar			
Shinsuke Nakamura			
Rey Mysterio			

BATTLE PACK SERIES 63 (2020)	MOC	LOOSE	VALUE
Bobby Lashley			
Finn Balor			
Brock Lesnar			
Seth Rollins			
Big E			
Xavier Woods			

BATTLE PACK SERIES 64 (2020)	MOC	LOOSE	VALUE
AJ Styles			
Daniel Bryan			
Lita			
Trish Stratus			
Jimmy Uso			
Jey Uso			

BATTLE PACK SERIES 65 (2020)	MOC	LOOSE	VALUE
Kevin Owens			
Ali			
Velveteen Dream			
Ricochet			
Matt Hardy			
Jeff Hardy			

BATTLE PACK SERIES 66 (2020)	MOC	LOOSE	VALUE
Drew McIntyre			
Shane McMahon			
Seth Rollins			
Becky Lynch			
The Undertaker			
Roman Reigns			

BATTLE PACK SERIES 67 (2020)	MOC	LOOSE	VALUE
Randy Orton			
Kofi Kingston			
Stone Cold Steve Austin			
AJ Styles			
John Morrison			
The Miz			

CHAMPIONSHIP SHOWDOWN SERIES 1 (2021)	MOC	LOOSE	VALUE
Roman Reigns			
Finn Balor			
Sasha Banks			
Alexa Bliss			
The Undertaker			
Jeff Hardy			

CHAMPIONSHIP SHOWDOWN SERIES 2 (2021)	MOC	LOOSE	VALUE
Bobby Lashley			
King Booker			
Randy Orton			
John Cena			
The Rock			
Triple H			

CHAMPIONSHIP SHOWDOWN SERIES 3 (2021)	MOC	LOOSE	VALUE
Kane			
Edge			
"The Fiend" Bray Wyatt			
Daniel Bryan			
The Giant			
Ric Flair			

CHAMPIONSHIP SHOWDOWN SERIES 4 (2021)	MOC	LOOSE	VALUE
Drew McIntyre			
Seth Rollins			
John Morrison			
Kofi Kingston			
Riddle			
AJ Styles			

CHAMPIONSHIP SHOWDOWN SERIES 5 (2021)	MOC	LOOSE	VALUE
British Bulldog			
Big Boss Man			
Chyna			
Trish Stratus			
Mankind			
Stone Cold Steve Austin			

CHAMPIONSHIP SHOWDOWN SERIES 6 (2021)	MOC	LOOSE	VALUE
Shawn Michaels			
John Cena			
Montez Ford			
Angelo Dawkins			
Jimmy Uso			
Jey Uso			

CHAMPIONSHIP SHOWDOWN SERIES 7 (2022)	MOC	LOOSE	VALUE
Rhea Ripley			
Charlotte Flair			
Cesaro			
Roman Reigns			
Kane			
Stone Cold Steve Austin			

CHAMPIONSHIP SHOWDOWN SERIES 8 (2022)	MOC	LOOSE	VALUE
Drew McIntyre			
Goldberg			
Angelo Dawkins			
Montez Ford			
Bret "Hit Man" Hart			
The Undertaker			

CHAMPIONSHIP SHOWDOWN SERIES 9 (2022)	MOC	LOOSE	VALUE
The Rock			
John Cena			
Sheamus			
Ricochet			
Bayley			
Sasha Banks			

CHAMPIONSHIP SHOWDOWN SERIES 10 (2022)	MOC	LOOSE	VALUE
Andre The Giant			
Hulk Hogan			
Bobby Lashley			
The Miz			
AJ Styles			
Omos			

CHAMPIONSHIP SHOWDOWN SERIES 11 (2023)	MOC	LOOSE	VALUE
Roman Reigns			
John Cena			
Becky Lynch			
Bianca Belair			
Jimmy Uso			
Jey Uso			

CHAMPIONSHIP SHOWDOWN SERIES 12 (2023)	MOC	LOOSE	VALUE
Bobby Lashley			
Big E			
Charlotte Flair			
Alexa Bliss			
Randy Orton			
Riddle			

CHAMPIONSHIP SHOWDOWN SERIES 13 (2023)	MOC	LOOSE	VALUE
Undertaker			
Batista			
Kofi Kingston			
Xavier Woods			
Ricochet			
Gunther			

CHAMPIONSHIP SHOWDOWN SERIES 14 (2023)	MOC	LOOSE	VALUE
Austin Theory			
Cody Rhodes			
Angelo Dawkins			
Montez Ford			
Mankind			
The Rock			

CHAMPIONSHIP SHOWDOWN SERIES 15 (2023)	MOC	LOOSE	VALUE
Kevin Owens			
AJ Styles			
Roman Reigns			
Logan Paul			
Stone Cold Steve Austin			
Triple H			

CHAMPIONSHIP SHOWDOWN SERIES 16 (2023)	MOC	LOOSE	VALUE
Brock Lesnar			
Bobby Lashley			
Shawn Michaels			
British Bulldog			
Ronda Rousey			
Liv Morgan			

MAIN EVENT SHOWDOWN SERIES 17 (2024)	MOC	LOOSE	VALUE
Gunther			
Rey Mysterio			
John Cena			
Austin Theory			
Roman Reigns			
Jey Uso			

MAIN EVENT SHOWDOWN SERIES 18 (2024)	MOC	LOOSE	VALUE
Bron Breakker			
Seth "Freakin'" Rollins			
Kane			
Mankind			
Rhea Ripley			
"Dirty" Dominik Mysterio			

MAIN EVENT SHOWDOWN SERIES 19 (2025)	MOC	LOOSE	VALUE
Hulk Hogan			
"Mean" Gene Okerlund			
John Cena			
The Rock			
Randy Orton			
CM Punk			

MAIN EVENT SHOWDOWN SERIES 20 (2025)	MOC	LOOSE	VALUE
Finn Bálor			
Damian Priest			
The Miz			
Gunther			
Stone Cold Steve Austin			
Kevin Owens			

MAIN EVENT SHOWDOWN SERIES 21 (2025)	MOC	LOOSE	VALUE
R-Truth			
"Dirty" Dominik Mysterio			
Roman Reigns			
LA Knight			
Xavier Woods			
Kofi Kingston			

MAIN EVENT SHOWDOWN SERIES 22 (2025)	MOC	LOOSE	VALUE
Cody Rhodes			
AJ Styles			
Austin Theory			
Grayson Waller			
Bianca Belair			
Jade Cargill			

MAIN EVENT SHOWDOWN SERIES 23 (2026)	MOC	LOOSE	VALUE
John Cena			
The Rock			
Jey Uso			
Drew McIntyre			
Seth Rollins			
CM Punk			

MAIN EVENT SHOWDOWN SERIES 24 (2026)	MOC	LOOSE	VALUE
Cody Rhodes			
Solo Sikoa			
LA Knight			
Logan Paul			
Tama Tonga			
Jacob Fatu			

MAIN EVENT SHOWDOWN SERIES 25 (2026)	MOC	LOOSE	VALUE

MAIN EVENT SHOWDOWN SERIES 26 (2026)	MOC	LOOSE	VALUE

2010 WRESTLEMANIA 26 2-PACKS	MOC	LOOSE	VALUE
Batista			
John Cena			
Big Show			
The Miz			
R-Truth			
John Morrison			

2014 WRESTLEMANIA 30 2-PACKS	MOC	LOOSE	VALUE
Brock Lesnar			
Batista			
Ultimate Warrior			
Sheamus			

2015 WRESTLEMANIA 31 2-PACKS	MOC	LOOSE	VALUE
Rey Mysterio			
Daniel Bryan			
Roman Reigns			
Triple H			

2016 WRESTLEMANIA 32 2-PACKS	MOC	LOOSE	VALUE
Ric Flair			
The Rock			
Stone Cold Steve Austin			
Bret Hart			

2016 SUMMERSLAM 2-PACKS	MOC	LOOSE	VALUE
John Cena			
Brock Lesnar			
Roman Reigns			
Dean Ambrose			

2017 WRESTLEMANIA 33 2-PACKS	MOC	LOOSE	VALUE
Andre The Giant			
Ted Dibiase			
The Rock			
John Cena			

2017 SUMMERSLAM 2-PACKS	MOC	LOOSE	VALUE
Randy Orton			
Brock Lesnar			
Ultimate Warrior			
Honky Tonk Man			

2018 WRESTLEMANIA 34 2-PACKS	MOC	LOOSE	VALUE
John Cena			
Nikki Bella			
Triple H			
Sting			
Roman Reigns			
The Undertaker			

2019 WRESTLEMANIA 35 2-PACKS	MOC	LOOSE	VALUE
Shinsuke Nakamura			
AJ Styles			
Edge			
Jeff Hardy			
Seth Rollins			
The Miz			

2020 WRESTLEMANIA 36 2-PACKS	MOC	LOOSE	VALUE
Roman Reigns			
Drew McIntyre			
Kane			
Daniel Bryan			
Randy Orton			
Rey Mysterio			

2015 THEN, NOW, FOREVER 2-PACKS (WALMART)	MOC	LOOSE	VALUE
Dean Ambrose			
Brian Pillman			
John Cena			
Stone Cold Steve Austin			
Ultimate Warrior			
Sting			

2017 FAN CENTRAL 2-PACKS (TOYS 'R' US)	MOC	LOOSE	VALUE
Seth Rollins			
Edge			
Sting			
The Undertaker			

114

2018 HALL OF CHAMPIONS 2-PACKS (TARGET)	MOC	LOOSE	VALUE
Dean Ambrose			
The Miz			
Batista			
John Cena			
Shawn Michaels			
Bret "Hitman" Hart			
Dash Wilder			
Scott Dawson			

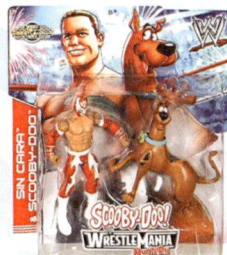

MISCELLANEOUS WWE 2-PACKS		MOC	LOOSE	VALUE
WWE 2K15 (K-MART)	Triple H			
	Shawn Michaels			
SCOOBY-DOO (KMART)	John Cena			
	Scooby-Doo			
	Sin Cara			
	Scooby-Doo			

RAW ON NETFLIX 2-PACKS	MOC	LOOSE	VALUE
Austin Theory			
John Cena			
British Bulldog			
Shawn Michaels			
Dominik Mysterio			
Rhea Ripley			
Stone Cold Steve Austin			
Triple H			

BASIC SERIES 1 COLLECTION BOX SET (TOYS 'R' US)	MIB	LOOSE	VALUE
Evan Bourne			
Big Show			
Triple H			
John Cena			
Batista			
Kofi Kingston			

ROYAL RUMBLE HERITAGE BOX SET (TOYS 'R' US)	MIB	LOOSE	VALUE
Christian			
John Cena			
Randy Orton			
Rey Mysterio			
Sheamus			
The Undertaker			

REY MYSTERIO COLLECTION BOX SET (TOYS 'R' US)		MIB	LOOSE	VALUE
JULY 1995	Rey Mysterio			
JUNE 1996	Rey Mysterio			
JULY 2002	Rey Mysterio			
JUNE 2003	Rey Mysterio			
FEB. 2005	Rey Mysterio			
DEC. 2005	Rey Mysterio			

CHAMPIONS COLLECTION BOX SET 1 (TARGET)	MIB	LOOSE	VALUE
Daniel Bryan			
John Cena			
Kane			
Dolph Ziggler			

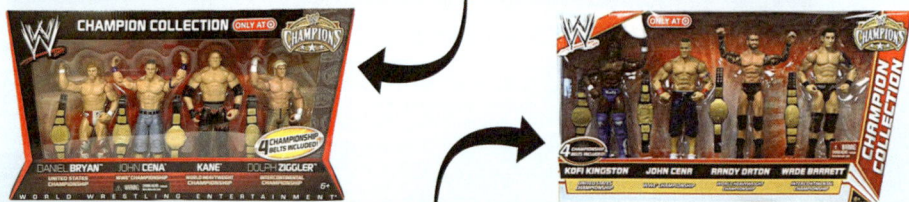

CHAMPIONS COLLECTION BOX SET 2 (TARGET)	MIB	LOOSE	VALUE
Kofi Kingston			
John Cena			
Randy Orton			
Wade Barrett			

CHAMPIONS COLLECTION BOX SET 3 (TARGET)	MIB	LOOSE	VALUE
Rey Mysterio			
The Rock			
Stone Cold Steve Austin			
John Cena			

2012 SUPERSTAR COLLECTION BOX SET 1 (WALMART)	MIB	LOOSE	VALUE
Rey Mysterio			
The Undertaker			
The Rock			
John Cena			
Sheamus			
Alberto Del Rio			

2012 SUPERSTAR COLLECTION BOX SET 2 (WALMART)	MIB	LOOSE	VALUE
Sin Cara			
Wade Barrett			
John Cena			
Randy Orton			
Brock Lesnar			
Alberto Del Rio			

2013 SUPERSTAR COLLECTION BOX SET 3 (WALMART)	MIB	LOOSE	VALUE
Sin Cara			
Rey Mysterio			
Daniel Bryan			
John Cena			
Alberto Del Rio			
Damien Sandow			

2013 SUPERSTAR COLLECTION BOX SET 4 (WALMART)	MIB	LOOSE	VALUE
Dean Ambrose			
Roman Reigns			
Seth Rollins			
Triple H			
Randy Orton			
Batista			

2014 WRESTLEMANIA BOX SET (WALMART)	MIB	LOOSE	VALUE
Mark Henry			
Triple H			
John Cena			
Randy Orton			
The Rock			
Brock Lesnar			

2014 FAN FAVORITES BOX SET (TOYS 'R' US)	MIB	LOOSE	VALUE
"Macho Man" Randy Savage			
Ultimate Warrior			
Shawn Michaels			
The Undertaker			
John Cena			
CM Punk			
Triple H			

2015 FAN FAVORITES BOX SET (K-MART)	MIB	LOOSE	VALUE
Dean Ambrose			
Seth Rollins			
Roman Reigns			
Rusev			
Cesaro			

2015 THEN, NOW, FOREVER BOX SET (WALMART)	MIB	LOOSE	VALUE
Andre The Giant			
Ric Flair			
Bret Hart			
John Cena			
Daniel Bryan			
Brock Lesnar			

2017 NETWORK SPOTLIGHT BOX SET 1 (TOYS 'R' US)	MIB	LOOSE	VALUE
Stone Cold Steve Austin			
Mr. McMahon			
Sting			
The Rock			
Ultimate Warrior			

2017 NETWORK SPOTLIGHT BOX SET 2 (TOYS 'R' US)	MIB	LOOSE	VALUE
Batista			
John Cena			
Kevin Nash			
Scott Hall			
Brock Lesnar			

UNDERTAKER COLLECTION BOX SET (TOYS 'R' US)		MIB	LOOSE	VALUE
1990	The Undertaker			
1994	The Undertaker			
1998	The Undertaker			
2014	The Undertaker			
2016	The Undertaker			

2023 MAIN EVENT SUPERSTARS BOX SET (SAM'S CLUB)	MIB	LOOSE	VALUE
Roman Reigns			
John Cena			
The Rock			

2024 MAIN EVENT SUPERSTARS BOX SET (SAM'S CLUB)	MIB	LOOSE	VALUE
Damian Priest			
Becky Lynch			
Seth Rollins			

2024 MAIN EVENT IMPERIUM BOX SET (SAM'S CLUB)	MIB	LOOSE	VALUE
Giovanni Vinci			
Gunther			
Ludwig Kaiser			

2025 MAIN EVENT BLOODLINE BOX SET (SMYTH'S)	MIB	LOOSE	VALUE
Jimmy Uso			
The Rock			
Roman Reigns			

2025 MAIN EVENT SUPERSTARS BOX SET (SMYTH'S)	MIB	LOOSE	VALUE
John Cena			
The Rock			
CM Punk			

2025 MAIN EVENT JUDGEMENT DAY BOX SET (SMYTH'S)	MIB	LOOSE	VALUE
Rhea Ripley			
Damian Priest			
Dominik Mysterio			

2025 MAIN EVENT SUPERSTARS BOX SET (SMYTH'S)	MIB	LOOSE	VALUE
Cody Rhodes			
Jey Uso			
Seth Freakin' Rollins			

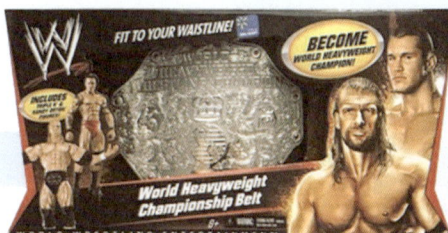

WWE CHAMPIONSHIP COMBO PACK BOX SETS (TOYS 'R' US)		MIB	LOOSE	VALUE
WWE TITLE COMBO PACK	John Cena			
	Edge			
WORLD TITLE COMBO PACK	Randy Orton			
	Triple H			

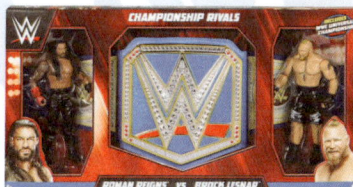

WWE CHAMPIONSHIP RIVALS BOX SETS (SAM'S CLUB)		MIB	LOOSE	VALUE
2022	Drew McIntyre			
	Randy Orton			
2023	Roman Reigns			
	Brock Lesnar			
2024	Roman Reigns			
	LA Knight			

ELITE COLLECTION

WWE ELITE COLLECTION SERIES 1 (2010)		MIB	LOOSE	VALUE
RAW – 1/19/2009	CM Punk			
ARMAGEDDON 2008	Edge			
	Jeff Hardy			
SMACKDOWN – 11/14/2008	MVP			
NO WAY OUT 2009	Rey Mysterio			
NO WAY OUT 2009	The Undertaker			

WWE ELITE COLLECTION SERIES 2 (2010)		MIB	LOOSE	VALUE
RAW – 10/13/2008	Batista			
WRESTLEMANIA 25	Matt Hardy			
ROYAL RUMBLE 2009	Randy Orton			
SMACKDOWN – 9/12/2008	R-Truth			
RAW – 6/15/2009	Ted Dibiase			
SMACKDOWN – 4/17/2009	Triple H			

WWE ELITE COLLECTION SERIES 3 (2010)		MIB	LOOSE	VALUE
WM 25/EXTREME RULES 2009	Christian			
BACKLASH 2009	Cody Rhodes			
SURVIVOR SERIES 2008	John Cena			
RAW – 2/23/2009	Santino Marella			
RAW – 9/22/2008	Shawn Michaels			
RAW – 4/13/2009	The Miz			

WWE ELITE COLLECTION SERIES 4 (2010)		MIB	LOOSE	VALUE
NIGHT OF CHAMPIONS 2009	Big Show			
UNFORGIVEN 2008	Chris Jericho (Blue Deco on Trunks)			
NO MERCY 2008	Chris Jericho (Purple Deco on Trunks)			
WRESTLEMANIA 25	Finlay			
JUDGEMENT DAY 2009	John Morrison (Maroon Coat)			
	John Morrison (Red Coat)			
RAW – 7/31/2009	Kane			
NIGHT OF CHAMPIONS 2009	Kofi Kingston			

WWE ELITE COLLECTION SERIES 5 (2010)		MIB	LOOSE	VALUE
UNFORGIVEN 2008	Chavo Guerrero			
SUMMERSLAM 2009	Dolph Ziggler			
RAW – 9/19/2009	Jack Swagger (Singlet Off)			
RAW – 7/13/2009	Jack Swagger (Singlet On)			
RAW – 8/3/2009	Mark Henry			
SMACKDOWN – 10/16/2009	Rey Mysterio			
ECW – 6/30/2009	Vladimir Kozlov (Logos On Coat)			
	Vladimir Kozlov (No Logos On Coat)			

WWE ELITE COLLECTION SERIES 6 (2010)		MIB	LOOSE	VALUE
RAW – 3/15/2009	Batista			
BREAKING POINT 2009	CM Punk			
ECW – 7/14/2009	Goldust			
SUMMERSLAM 2009	JTG			
SMACKDOWN – 10/30/2009	Matt Hardy			
RAW – 1/5/2009	Shad			

WWE ELITE COLLECTION SERIES 7 (2011)		MIB	LOOSE	VALUE
SMACKDOWN – 9/18/2009	David Hart Smith			
RAW – 12/29/2009	Hornswoggle			
SURVIVOR SERIES 2009	John Cena			
SURVIVOR SERIES 2009	Shawn Michaels			
BREAKING POINT 2009	Triple H			
SMACKDOWN – 9/18/2009	Tyson Kidd			

WWE ELITE COLLECTION SERIES 8 (2011)		MIB	LOOSE	VALUE
WRESTLEMANIA XXVI	Drew McIntyre			
WRESTLEMANIA XXVI	Edge			
RAW – 5/31/2009	Evan Bourne			
TLC 2009	Sheamus			
SURVIVOR SERIES 2009	The Undertaker			
RAW – 5/11/2009	William Regal			

WWE ELITE COLLECTION SERIES 9 (2011)		MIB	LOOSE	VALUE
ROYAL RUMBLE 2010	Kofi Kingston			
SUMMERSLAM 2010	Luke Gallows			
WRESTLEMANIA XXVI	MVP			
EXTREME RULES 2009	Randy Orton			
WRESTLEMANIA XXVI	The Miz			
SUPERSTARS – 11/19/2009	Zack Ryder			

WWE ELITE COLLECTION SERIES 10 (2011)		MIB	LOOSE	VALUE
RAW – 3/22/2010	Big Show			
SUMMERSLAM 2010	John Morrison			
MONEY IN THE BANK 2010	Kane			
OVER THE LIMIT 2010	R-Truth			
SURVIVOR SERIES 2010	Ted Dibiase (Green Trunks)			
ROYAL RUMBLE 2011	Ted Dibiase (Purple Trunks)			
ROYAL RUMBLE 2010	Yoshi Tatsu			

WWE ELITE COLLECTION SERIES 11 (2011)		MIB	LOOSE	VALUE
RAW – 4/26/2010	Christian			
NIGHT OF CHAMPIONS 2010	CM Punk			
SUMMERSLAM 2010	John Cena			
EXTREME RULES 2010	Rey Mysterio			
ELIMINATION CHAMBER 2011	The Miz			
RAW – 7/12/2010	Wade Barrett			

WWE ELITE COLLECTION SERIES 12 (2012)		MIB	LOOSE	VALUE
SMACKDOWN – 8/20/2010	Alberto Del Rio			
HELL IN A CELL 2010	Daniel Bryan			
ROYAL RUMBLE 2011	Justin Gabriel			
BADD BLOOD: IN YOUR HOUSE	Kane			
SUPERSTARS – 2/8/1992	Papa Shango			
ROYAL RUMBLE 2011	Randy Orton			

WWE ELITE COLLECTION SERIES 13 (2012)		MIB	LOOSE	VALUE
SMACKDOWN – 9/8/2010	Big Show			
WRESTLEMANIA XXVII	Cody Rhodes (Jacket Off)			
	Cody Rhodes (Jacket On)			
RAW – 5/30/2011	Dolph Ziggler			
RAW IS WAR – 5/24/1999	Edge			
SMACKDOWN – 1/7/2011	Rey Mysterio			
TLC 2010	Sheamus			

WWE ELITE COLLECTION SERIES 14 (2012)		MIB	LOOSE	VALUE
SUMMERSLAM 2011	Alberto Del Rio			
SURVIVOR SERIES 1988	Big Boss Man			
SMACKDOWN – 6/30/2006	Booker T			
SUMMERSLAM 2011	John Cena			
RAW – 4/4/2011	The Rock			
WRESTLEMANIA XXVI	The Undertaker			

WWE ELITE COLLECTION SERIES 15 (2012)		MIB	LOOSE	VALUE
NIGHT OF CHAMPIONS 2011	Evan Bourne			
NIGHT OF CHAMPIONS 2011	Mark Henry			
RAW – 10/10/2011	R-Truth			
SUMMERSLAM 2009	Rey Mysterio			
SMACKDOWN – 8/12/2011	Sin Cara (Gold)			
	Sin Cara (Yellow)			
KING OF THE RING 1993	Yokozuna			

WWE ELITE COLLECTION SERIES 16 (2012)		MIB	LOOSE	VALUE
MONEY IN THE BANK 2011	CM Punk			
IN YOUR HOUSE 1 1995	Diesel			
SMACKDOWN – 12/9/2011	Ezekiel Jackson			
MONEY IN THE BANK 2011	Heath Slater			
SPRING STAMPEDE 1999	Kevin Nash			
SMACKDOWN – 5/6/2011	Randy Orton			
RAW – 11/14/2011	The Rock			

WWE ELITE COLLECTION SERIES 17 (2012)		MIB	LOOSE	VALUE
VENGEANCE 2011	John Cena			
NIGHT OF CHAMPIONS 2011	Kelly Kelly			
NIGHT OF CHAMPIONS 2011	Kofi Kingston			
RAW – 4/12/1999	Mankind			
WRESTLEMANIA XXVII	Sheamus			
VENGEANCE 2011	Zack Ryder			

WWE ELITE COLLECTION SERIES 18 (2013)		MIB	LOOSE	VALUE
RAW – 1/9/2012	Brodus Clay			
WRESTLEMANIA XXVII	Jerry "The King" Lawler			
NO MERCY 2007	Rey Mysterio			
MONEY IN THE BANK 2011	Sin Cara			
JUDGEMENT DAY 2002	The Undertaker			
SMACKDOWN 2/17/2012	Wade Barrett			

WWE ELITE COLLECTION SERIES 19 (2013)		MIB	LOOSE	VALUE
EXTREME RULES 2012	Brock Lesnar			
RAW SUPERSHOW – 5/21/2012	Daniel Bryan			
ELIMINATION CHAMBER 2012	Dolph Ziggler			
RAW – 12/12/2011	Kane			
WRESTLEMANIA IV	Miss Elizabeth			
BADD BLOOD: IN YOUR HOUSE	Shawn Michaels			

WWE ELITE COLLECTION SERIES 20 (2013)		MIB	LOOSE	VALUE
WRESTLEMANIA XXVIII	Chris Jericho			
WRESTLEMANIA X7	Christian			
CAPITOL PUNISHMENT 2011	CM Punk			
WRESTLEMANIA XXVIII	Cody Rhodes			
MONEY IN THE BANK 2012	John Cena			
SMACKDOWN – 3/5/2012	Santino Marella			

WWE ELITE COLLECTION SERIES 21 (2013)		MIB	LOOSE	VALUE
SMACKDOWN 9/16/2011	AJ Lee			
SUMMERSLAM 2012	Alberto Del Rio			
SUMMERSLAM 1989	Honky Tonk Man			
SMACKDOWN – 3/16/2012	Randy Orton			
RAW 1000	Rey Mysterio			
NO WAY OUT 2012	Ryback			

WWE ELITE COLLECTION SERIES 22 (2013)		MIB	LOOSE	VALUE
HELL IN A CELL 2012	Big Show			
SMACKDOWN – 5/25/2012	Damien Sandow			
THE GREAT AMERICAN BASH 1998	The Giant			
NIGHT OF CHAMPIONS 2012	Kane			
RAW SUPERSHOW – 4/2/2012	Tensai			
ELIMINATION CHAMBER 2013	The Rock			

WWE ELITE COLLECTION SERIES 23 (2013)		MIB	LOOSE	VALUE
HELL IN A CELL 2012	Antonio Cesaro			
WRESTLEMANIA 21	JBL			
SURVIVOR SERIES 2012	John Cena			
WRESTLEMANIA VIII	"Macho Man" Randy Savage			
WRESTLEMANIA XV	Triple H			
SURVIVOR SERIES 1995	The Undertaker			

WWE ELITE COLLECTION SERIES 24 (2013)		MIB	LOOSE	VALUE
RAW – 4/8/2013	Dolph Ziggler			
RAW – 10/29/2012	Rey Mysterio			
HELL IN A CELL 2012	Ryback			
TLC 2012	The Miz			
SURVIVOR SERIES 2005	Trish Stratus			
RAW – 12/20/2012	Wade Barrett			

WWE ELITE COLLECTION SERIES 25 (2014)		MIB	LOOSE	VALUE
RAW – 1/14/2013	Brodus Clay			
CIRCA 1970	Bruno Sammartino			
ELIMINATION CHAMBER 2013	Dean Ambrose			
TLC 2012	Seth Rollins			
SURVIVOR SERIES 2012	Sheamus			
RAW – 2/18/2013	Sin Cara			

WWE ELITE COLLECTION SERIES 26 (2014)		MIB	LOOSE	VALUE
RAW SUPERSHOW – 1/28/2013	Big E Langston			
WRESTLEMANIA 29	Jack Swagger			
WRESTLEMANIA 29	Mark Henry			
RAW – 4/9/1999	Road Dogg			
RAW – 4/1/2013	Roman Reigns			
SUMMERSLAM 1992	Ultimate Warrior			

WWE ELITE COLLECTION SERIES 27 (2014)		MIB	LOOSE	VALUE
RAW – 7/27/1998	Billy Gunn			
EXTREME RULES 2013	Fandango			
SMACKDOWN – 10/4/2013	Kofi Kingston			
SMACKDOWN – 10/10/2002	Rikishi (Sarong On)			
WRESTLEMANIA 2000	Rikishi (Sarong Off)			
RAW – 7/13/2013	Rob Van Dam			
WRESTLEMANIA XXVIII	The Undertaker			

WWE ELITE COLLECTION SERIES 28 (2014)		MIB	LOOSE	VALUE
RAW – 8/19/2013	Big Show			
SMACKDOWN – 9/27/2013	Bray Wyatt			
ROYAL RUMBLE 2013	Daniel Bryan			
SUMMERSLAM 1990	Demolition Crush			
ROYAL RUMBLE 2014	John Cena			
EXTREME RULES 2013	Triple H			

WWE ELITE COLLECTION SERIES 29 (2014)		MIB	LOOSE	VALUE
WRESTLEMANIA III	Andre The Giant			
RAW – 8/26/2013	CM Punk			
MONEY IN THE BANK 2013	Damien Sandow			
SMACKDOWN – 7/26/2013	Erick Rowan			
SMACKDOWN – 11/3/2013	Goldust			
SMACKDOWN – 8/16/2013	Luke Harper			

WWE ELITE COLLECTION SERIES 30 (2014)		MIB	LOOSE	VALUE
BATTLE ROYAL AT THE ALBERT HALL	Animal			
ROYAL RUMBLE 2014	Batista (Facing Backward)			
ROYAL RUMBLE 2014	Batista (Facing Forward)			
RAW – 2/24/2014	Brock Lesnar			
BATTLE ROYAL AT THE ALBERT HALL	Hawk			
RAW – 6/27/1994	Lex Luger			
RAW – 9/16/2013	Ryback			

WWE ELITE COLLECTION SERIES 31 (2014)		MIB	LOOSE	VALUE
WRESTLEMANIA XXX	Dean Ambrose			
RAW – 9/16/2013	Jey Uso			
RAW – 9/16/2013	Jimmy Uso			
RAW – 10/28/2013	Kane			
RAW – 3/24/2003 & BACKLASH 2003	The Rock			
SUMMERSLAM 1996	Vader			

WWE ELITE COLLECTION SERIES 32 (2015)		MIB	LOOSE	VALUE
WRESTLEMANIA 29	Big E			
ROYAL RUMBLE 2014	Cody Rhodes			
ROYAL RUMBLE 2014	Daniel Bryan			
RAW – 2/10/2014	Mark Henry			
STARRCADE 1996	Rey Mysterio			
MAIN EVENT – 4/8/2014	Sin Cara			

WWE ELITE COLLECTION SERIES 33 (2015)		MIB	LOOSE	VALUE
PAYBACK 2014	Batista			
RAW – 4/1/2014	Cesaro			
WRESTLEMANIA III	Junkyard Dog			
WRESTLEMANIA XXX	Roman Reigns			
WRESTLEMANIA XXX	Seth Rollins			
WRESTLEMANIA 2000	X-Pac			

WWE ELITE COLLECTION SERIES 34 (2015)		MIB	LOOSE	VALUE
RAW – 4/7/2014	Bad News Barrett			
WRESTLEMANIA IX	Doink The Clown			
RAW – 2/24/2014	Hulk Hogan			
SMACKDOWN – 4/11/2014	John Cena			
RAW – 4/7/2014	Paige			
PAYBACK 2014	Rusev			

WWE ELITE COLLECTION SERIES 35 (2015)		MIB	LOOSE	VALUE
SMACKDOWN – 5/9/2014	Diego			
ROYAL RUMBLE 1991	Earthquake			
SMACKDOWN – 5/9/2014	Fernando			
WRESTLEMANIA XXX	Luke Harper			
BATTLEGROUND 2014	Randy Orton			
WRESTLEMANIA XXX	Triple H			

WWE ELITE COLLECTION SERIES 36 (2015)		MIB	LOOSE	VALUE
RAW – 6/23/2014	Bo Dallas			
SUMMERSLAM 2014	Bray Wyatt			
RAW – 7/21/2014	Dean Ambrose			
NITRO – 2/24/1997	Diamond Dallas Page			
HELL IN A CELL 2014	Goldust			
HELL IN A CELL 2014	Stardust			

WWE ELITE COLLECTION SERIES 37 (2015)		MIB	LOOSE	VALUE
NIGHT OF CHAMPIONS 2014	Brock Lesnar			
NITRO – 6/5/1996	Dean Malenko			
NIGHT OF CHAMPIONS 2014	John Cena			
SMACKDOWN – 8/29/2014	Seth Rollins			
SUMMERSLAM 2014	Stephanie McMahon			
TLC 2014	The Miz			

WWE ELITE COLLECTION SERIES 38 (2015)		MIB	LOOSE	VALUE
SMACKDOWN – 6/20/2014	Adam Rose			
RAW – 4/10/2000	Bradshaw (Sleeves)			
RAW – 4/10/2000	Bradshaw (No Sleeves)			
EXTREME RULES 2014	Daniel Bryan			
RAW – 4/10/2000	Faarooq (Sleeves)			
RAW – 4/10/2000	Faarooq (No Sleeves)			
BASH AT THE BEACH 1995	"Macho Man" Randy Savage			
RAW – 4/7/14 & HELL IN A CELL 2014	Roman Reigns			

WWE ELITE COLLECTION SERIES 39 (2016)		MIB	LOOSE	VALUE
WWF ON TELECINCO – 10/10/1991	British Bulldog			
TLC 2014	Damien Mizdow			
RAW – 12/29/2014	Dolph Ziggler			
RAW – 1/19/2015	Sting			
SURVIVOR SERIES 1996	Sycho Sid			
ROCK BOTTOM: IN YOUR HOUSE	The Godfather			

WWE ELITE COLLECTION SERIES 40 (2016)		MIB	LOOSE	VALUE
SURVIVOR SERIES 1992	Irwin R. Schyster			
WRESTLEMANIA 31	John Cena			
WRESTLEMANIA IV	"Ravishing" Rick Rude			
NXT TAKEOVER: REVIVAL	Sami Zayn			
FASTLANE 2015	Tyson Kidd			
THE GREAT AMERICAN BASH 2007	Umaga			

WWE ELITE COLLECTION SERIES 41 (2016)		MIB	LOOSE	VALUE
RAW – 1/10/1994	1-2-3 Kid			
RAW – 5/25/2015	Dean Ambrose			
NXT TAKEOVER: REVIVAL	Finn Bálor			
RAW – 10/30/2000	Lita			
WRESTLEMANIA 31	Ryback			
ECW BARELY LEGAL 1997	Terry Funk			

WWE ELITE COLLECTION SERIES 42 (2016)		MIB	LOOSE	VALUE
RAW – 5/28/2015	Kalisto			
RAW – 3/15/1993	Brian Knobbs			
RAW – 3/15/1993	Jerry Sags			
RAW – 3/30/2015	Neville			
WRESTLEMANIA 31	Triple H			
ELIMINATION CHAMBER 2015	Xavier Woods			

WWE ELITE COLLECTION SERIES 43 (2016)		MIB	LOOSE	VALUE
HELL IN A CELL 2015	Alberto Del Rio			
SUMMERSLAM 1990	Bret "Hit Man" Hart			
SUMMERSLAM 1990	Jim "The Anvil" Neidhart			
RAW – 6/8/2015	Kevin Owens			
ELIMINATION CHAMBER 2015	Kofi Kingston			
NXT – 6/10/2015	Samoa Joe			

WWE ELITE COLLECTION SERIES 44 (2016)		MIB	LOOSE	VALUE
ELIMINATION CHAMBER 2015	Big E			
RAW – 8/24/2015	Braun Strowman			
SAT. NIGHT MAIN EVENT – 11/14/1992	"Macho Man" Randy Savage			
BATTLEGROUND 2015	Sasha Banks			
SMACKDOWN – 5/28/2015	Sin Cara			
SUPERSTARS – 1/27/1990	Tugboat			

WWE ELITE COLLECTION SERIES 45 (2016)		MIB	LOOSE	VALUE
RAW – 8/31/2015	Bubba Ray Dudley			
RAW – 8/31/2015	D-Von Dudley			
NITRO – 11/26/1996	Lord Steven Regal			
ROYAL RUMBLE 1993	Lex Luger			
HELL IN A CELL 2015	Roman Reigns			
SUMMERSLAM 2015	Seth Rollins			

WWE ELITE COLLECTION SERIES 46 (2017)		MIB	LOOSE	VALUE
NITRO – 7/15/1996	Booker T			
THE BEAST IN THE EAST	Finn Bálor			
SUMMERSLAM 2015	John Cena			
RAW – 11/30/2015	Rusev			
RAW – 3/30/2015	Sheamus			
NITRO – 7/15/1996	Stevie Ray			

WWE ELITE COLLECTION SERIES 47A (2017)		MIB	LOOSE	VALUE
ROYAL RUMBLE 2016	AJ Styles			
NXT TAKEOVER: RESPECT	Asuka			
RAW – 10/12/1998	Big Boss Man			
SMACKDOWN – 10/29/2015	Cesaro			
RAW – 10/19/2015	Kevin Owens			
SUPERSTARS – 6/27/1992	Tatanka			

WWE ELITE COLLECTION SERIES 47B (2017)		MIB	LOOSE	VALUE
HALLOWEEN HAVOC 1991	Brian Pillman			
IN YOUR HOUSE 4: GREAT WHITE NORTH	Goldust			
HELL IN A CELL 2015	Kane			
ROYAL RUMBLE 2016	Konnor			
UNFORGIVEN 2000	The Rock			
ROYAL RUMBLE 2016	Viktor			

WWE ELITE COLLECTION SERIES 48 (2017)		MIB	LOOSE	VALUE
SMACKDOWN – 11/10/2006	The Boogeyman			
IWA KAWASAKI DREAM – 8/20/1995	Cactus Jack			
EXTREME RULES 2016	Dean Ambrose			
SURVIVOR SERIES 2015	Dolph Ziggler			
ROYAL RUMBLE 2016	Erick Rowan			
FASTLANE 2016	Kalisto			

WWE ELITE COLLECTION SERIES 49 (2017)		MIB	LOOSE	VALUE
NXT TAKEOVER LONDON	Apollo Crews			
ROYAL RUMBLE 2016	Becky Lynch			
RAW – 4/4/2016	Big Cass			
WRESTLING CHALLENGE – 2/5/1989	Brutus "The Barber" Beefcake			
ROADBLOCK 2016	Enzo Amore			
WRESTLEMANIA 21	Randy Orton			

WWE ELITE COLLECTION SERIES 50 (2017)		MIB	LOOSE	VALUE
NXT TAKEOVER DALLAS	Baron Corbin			
SUMMERSLAM 2016	John Cena			
SMACKDOWN – 8/30/2016	Rhyno			
WRESTLEMANIA 32	Shane McMahon			
WRESTLEMANIA 32	Stephanie McMahon			
WRESTLEMANIA VII	Warlord			

WWE ELITE COLLECTION SERIES 51 (2017)		MIB	LOOSE	VALUE
BACKLASH 2016	AJ Styles			
WRESTLING CHALLENGE – 2/16/1991	Berzerker			
SUMMERSLAM 1997	Mankind			
SUMMERSLAM 2016	Roman Reigns			
RAW – 11/21/2016	Sami Zayn			
BASH AT THE BEACH 1996	Scott Hall			

WWE ELITE COLLECTION SERIES 52 (2017)		MIB	LOOSE	VALUE
RAW – 11/21/2016	Braun Strowman			
RAW – 7/6/1998	D'Lo Brown			
IN YOUR HOUSE 15: A COLD DAY IN HELL	Ken Shamrock			
CLASH OF CHAMPIONS 2016	Kofi Kingston			
SUMMERSLAM 2016	Seth Rollins			
CLASH OF CHAMPIONS 2016	Xavier Woods			

WWE ELITE COLLECTION SERIES 53 (2017)		MIB	LOOSE	VALUE
BACKLASH 2016	Alexa Bliss			
CLASH OF CHAMPIONS 2016	Big E			
MONEY IN THE BANK 2016	Chris Jericho			
NO MERCY 2016	Heath Slater			
CLASH OF CHAMPIONS 2016	Kevin Owens			
SUMMERSLAM 2016	The Miz			

WWE ELITE COLLECTION SERIES 54 (2018)		MIB	LOOSE	VALUE
ELIMINATION CHAMBER 2017	Bray Wyatt			
WRESTLEMANIA 32	Charlotte Flair			
SMACKDOWN – 9/13/2016	Jey Uso			
SMACKDOWN – 9/13/2016	Jimmy Uso			
SMACKDOWN – 1/31/2017	John Cena			
RAW – 12/26/2016	Rich Swann			

WWE ELITE COLLECTION SERIES 55 (2018)		MIB	LOOSE	VALUE
WRESTLEMANIA 33	Big Cass			
WRESTLEMANIA 33	Brock Lesnar			
RAW – 6/27/2016	Enzo Amore			
SMACKDOWN – 12/20/2016	James Ellsworth			
WRESTLEMANIA 33	Neville			
WRESTLEMANIA XIX	The Undertaker			

WWE ELITE COLLECTION SERIES 56 (2018)		MIB	LOOSE	VALUE
SURVIVOR SERIES 2016	AJ Styles			
205 LIVE – 11/29/2016	Gentleman Jack Gallagher			
ROYAL RUMBLE 2017	Karl Anderson			
HELL IN A CELL 2016	Luke Gallows			
FASTLANE 2017	Roman Reigns			
EXTREME RULES 2017	Samoa Joe			

WWE ELITE COLLECTION SERIES 57 (2018)		MIB	LOOSE	VALUE
MONEY IN THE BANK 2017	Baron Corbin			
WRESTLEMANIA 33	Jeff Hardy			
SMACKDOWN – 12/16/1999	Scotty 2 Hotty			
WRESTLEMANIA 33	Seth Rollins			
BACKLASH 2017	Shinsuke Nakamura			
NXT TAKEOVER TORONTO	Tye Dillinger			

WWE ELITE COLLECTION SERIES 58 (2018)		MIB	LOOSE	VALUE
GREAT BALLS OF FIRE 2017	Braun Strowman			
WRESTLEMANIA 33	Cesaro			
EXTREME RULES 2017	Dean Ambrose			
PAYBACK 2017	Matt Hardy			
NXT TAKEOVER TORONTO	Mickie James			
WRESTLEMANIA 33	Sheamus			

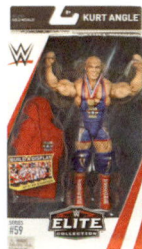

WWE ELITE COLLECTION SERIES 59 (2018)		MIB	LOOSE	VALUE
SMACKDOWN – 12/27/2016	Chad Gable			
RAW – 8/15/2016	Finn Bálor			
SMACKDOWN – 12/27/2016	Jason Jordan			
WRESTLEMANIA XIX	Kurt Angle			
WRESLEMANIA 33	The Miz			
BATTLEGROUND 2016	Zack Ryder			

WWE ELITE COLLECTION SERIES 60 (2018)		MIB	LOOSE	VALUE
NXT – 11/17/2016	Elias			
PRIME TIME WRESTLING – 9/8/1986	Giant Machine			
SMACKDOWN – 7/18/2017	John Cena			
SMACKDOWN – 7/4/2017	Kofi Kingston			
WRESTLEMANIA 33	Triple H			
SMACKDOWN – 7/4/2017	Xavier Woods			

WWE ELITE COLLECTION SERIES 61 (2018)		MIB	LOOSE	VALUE
SUMMERSLAM 2017	AJ Styles			
SMACKDOWN – 7/4/2017	BIG E			
SMACKDOWN – 10/10/2017	Fandango			
SMACKDOWN – 8/1/2017	Kevin Owens			
HELL IN A CELL 2017	Shane McMahon			
SMACKDOWN – 10/10/2017	Tyler Breeze			

WWE ELITE COLLECTION SERIES 62 (2018)		MIB	LOOSE	VALUE
NXT TAKEOVER ORLANDO	Akam			
TLC 2017	Braun Strowman			
RAW – 7/14/1997	Dude Love			
NXT TAKEOVER ORLANDO	Rezar			
ROYAL RUMBLE 2018	Roman Reigns			
GREAT AMERICAN BASH 1991	Sting			

WWE ELITE COLLECTION SERIES 63 (2019)		MIB	LOOSE	VALUE
SURVIVOR SERIES 1994	Bob Backlund (Walmart)			
TLC 2017	Dean Ambrose			
SUPERSTARS – 2/7/1986	Dusty Rhodes			
ROYAL RUMBLE 2018	Kane			
SMACKDOWN – 11/14/2017	Sami Zayn			
SMACKDOWN – 8/29/2017	Shelton Benjamin (Standard - Bald)			
WRESTLEMANIA 25	Shelton Benjamin (Chase - Gold Standard)			
NXT TAKEOVER ORLANDO	Shinsuke Nakamura			

WWE ELITE COLLECTION SERIES 64 (2019)		MIB	LOOSE	VALUE
ELIMINATION CHAMBER 2017	Curt Hawkins (Standard - Blue Singlet)			
RAW – 9/25/2017	Curt Hawkins (Chase - Black Singlet)			
HELL IN A CELL 2017	Jey Uso			
HELL IN A CELL 2017	Jimmy Uso			
RAW – 1/22/2018	John Cena			
NXT TAKEOVER CHICAGO	Pete Dunne (Target)			
RAW – 3/13/2017	Samoa Joe			
ROYAL RUMBLE 2018	Seth Rollins			

WWE ELITE COLLECTION SERIES 65 (2019)		MIB	LOOSE	VALUE
CLASH OF CHAMPIONS 2017	Aiden English (Standard – Black Tights)			
SMACKDOWN – 8/22/2017	Aiden English (Chase - Grey on Tights)			
NXT – 4/19/2017	Eric Young			
RAW – 12/11/2017	Nia Jax			
RAW – 11/20/2017	Roman Reigns			
ELIMINATION CHAMBER 2018	Ronda Rousey			
CLASH OF CHAMPIONS 2017	Rusev			
WRESTLEMANIA VI	Sensational Sherri (Walmart)			

WWE ELITE COLLECTION SERIES 66 (2019)		MIB	LOOSE	VALUE
ROYAL RUMBLE 2018	AJ Styles			
NXT – 4/19/2017	Alexander Wolfe (Target)			
SMACKDOWN – 11/21/2017	Harper			
ROYAL RUMBLE 2018	Kevin Owens (Standard - Fight Anyone Shirt)			
WRESTLEMANIA 34	Kevin Owens (Chase - KO-Mania III Shirt)			
SURVIVOR SERIES 2017	Kurt Angle			
NXT – 4/19/2017	Nikki Cross			
SMACKDOWN – 11/21/2017	Rowan			

WWE ELITE COLLECTION SERIES 67 (2019)		MIB	LOOSE	VALUE
WRESTLEMANIA 34	Cedric Alexander			
SMACKDOWN – 7/10/2018	Jeff Hardy (Standard - Blue Camo Sleeves)			
SMACKDOWN – 7/3/2018	Jeff Hardy (Chase - Blue Sleeves)			
SMACKDOWN – 4/3/2018	Randy Orton			
HALLOWEEN HAVOC 1997	Rey Mysterio			
NXT TAKEOVER NEW ORLEANS	Shayna Baszler			
NXT – 5/25/2017	Velveteen Dream			

WWE ELITE COLLECTION SERIES 68 - SUMMERSLAM (2019)		MIB	LOOSE	VALUE
SUMMERSLAM 2018	Braun Strowman			
SUMMERSLAM 2014	Brie Bella			
SUMMERSLAM 2018	Daniel Bryan			
RAW – 6/26/1995	King Mabel (Standard - M On Chest)			
SUMMERSLAM 1995	King Mabel (Chase - Lightning Bolts)			
RAW – 5/10/1999	Pat Patterson (Walmart)			
SUMMERSLAM 2018	Roman Reigns			
SUMMERSLAM 2000	The Undertaker			

WWE ELITE COLLECTION SERIES 69 (2019)

		MIB	LOOSE	VALUE
SUPER SHOWDOWN 2019	Ali (Standard - Yellow Tights)			
WRESTLEMANIA 35	Ali (Chase - Red Tights)			
RAW – 4/16/2018	Bobby Lashley			
ROYAL RUMBLE 2018	Liv Morgan (Target)			
SMACKDOWN – 1/22/2019	Rey Mysterio			
NXT TAKEOVER CHICAGO II	Ricochet			
EVOLUTION	Sonya Deville (Target)			
WRESTLEMANIA 34	The Miz			
KING OF THE RING 2000	The Rock (Walmart)			
NXT TAKEOVER CHICAGO II	Tommaso Ciampa			

WWE ELITE COLLECTION SERIES 70 (2019)

		MIB	LOOSE	VALUE
SUMMERSLAM 2018	Dolph Ziggler (Standard - Black Tights)			
FASTLANE 2018	Dolph Ziggler (Chase - Pink Tights)			
NAT – 5/9/2018	EC3			
NXT TAKEOVER LONDON	Finn Bálor			
RAW – 5/10/1999	Gerald Brisco (Walmart)			
NXT TAKEOVER BROOKLYN IV	Johnny Gargano			
SUPERSTARS – 9/22/1990	Mr. McMahon			
SUPER SHOWDOWN 2018	Seth Rollins			

WWE ELITE COLLECTION SERIES 71 (2019)

		MIB	LOOSE	VALUE
NZT – 6/27/2018	Adam Cole			
SURVIVOR SERIES 1999	Big Show			
HELL IN A CELL 2018	Drew McIntyre			
SMACKDOWN – 7/24/2018	Jeff Hardy			
RAW – 1/7/2019	John Cena			
NXT TAKEOVER PHILADELPHIA	Kassius Ohno (Target)			
EVOLUTION	Nikki Bella (Standard - Bellalution Shirt)			
SMACKDOWN – 3/7/2017	Nikki Bella (Chase - Do More, Fear Less Shirt)			
RAW – 12/11/2017	Paige (Target)			

WWE ELITE COLLECTION SERIES 72 (2020)		MIB	LOOSE	VALUE
WRESTLEMANIA 35	Batista			
SMACKDOWN – 1/1/2019	Becky Lynch			
SURVIVOR SERIES 2018	Buddy Murphy (Standard - Red Gear)			
205 LIVE – 3/27/2018	Buddy Murphy (Chase - Black Gear)			
SURVIVOR SERIES 1987	Gorilla Monsoon (Walmart)			
SMACKDOWN 1000 – 10/16/2018	Rey Mysterio			
NXT TAKEOVER WAR GAMES	Roderick Strong			
NXT – 10/2/2019	Velveteen Dream			

WWE ELITE COLLECTION SERIES 73 (2020)		MIB	LOOSE	VALUE
NXT TAKEOVER WAR GAMES 2018	Aleister Black			
SMACKDOWN – 2/5/2019	Daniel Bryan			
MONEY IN THE BANK 2018	Elias			
RAW – 9/19/2016	Gran Metalik (Standard - Blue Gear)			
205 LIVE – 1/23/2018	Gran Metalik (Chase - Black Gear)			
NXT TAKEOVER BROOKLYN IV	Kairi Sane			
SMACKDOWN – 5/8/2018	Peyton Royce (Target)			
WRESTLEMANIA 34	Triple H			

WWE ELITE COLLECTION SERIES 74 (2020)		MIB	LOOSE	VALUE
ROYAL RUMBLE 2019	AJ Styles			
ROYAL RUMBLE 2019	Andrade			
ROYAL RUMBLE 2019	Finn Bálor			
RAW – 10/29/2003	Goldberg			
SURVIVOR SERIES 1994	Jim "The Anvil" Neidhart (Walmart)			
205 LIVE – 6/5/2018	Lince Dorado (Standard - Black Tights)			
RAW – 1/7/2019	Lince Dorado (Chase - Gold Tights)			
ROYAL RUMBLE 2018	Natalya			

WWE ELITE COLLECTION SERIES 75 (2020)		MIB	LOOSE	VALUE
ELIMINATION CHAMBER 2019	Billie Kay (Target)			
2002	Jeff Hardy			
RAW – 2/4/2019	Kalisto			
SMACKDOWN – 2/19/2019	Mandy Rose			
NXT TAKEOVER BLACKPOOL	Pete Dunne			
ROYAL RUMBLE 2019	Seth Rollins			
SMACKDOWN 5/9/2002	The Hurricane (Standard - Black Boots)			
RAW – 3/10/2003	The Hurricane (Chase - White Boots)			

WWE ELITE COLLECTION SERIES 76 (2020)		MIB	LOOSE	VALUE
WRESTLEMANIA 35	Braun Strowman			
JUDGEMENT DAY 1998	Christian (Standard - White Shirt)			
RAW – 7/26/1999	Christian (Chase - Black Shirt)			
WRESTLEMANIA 35	John Cena			
RAW – 4/29/2019	Lacey Evans			
EXTREME RULES 2019	Otis			
EXTREME RULES 2019	Tucker			

WWE ELITE COLLECTION SERIES 77 - SUMMERSLAM (2020)		MIB	LOOSE	VALUE
SUMMERSLAM 2019	AJ Styles			
WRESTLEMANIA	"Classy" Freddie Blassie (Walmart)			
SUMMERSLAM 1988	Miss Elizabeth			
SUMMERSLAM 1989	"Ravishing" Rick Rude (Standard - Warrior Tights)			
SUPERSTARS – 4/2/1989	"Ravishing" Rick Rude (Chase - IC Title Tights)			
SUMMERSLAM 2018	Ronda Rousey			
SUMMERSLAM 2019	"The Fiend" Bray Wyatt			
SUMMERSLAM 1999	Viscera			

WWE ELITE COLLECTION SERIES 78 (2020)		MIB	LOOSE	VALUE
RAW – 7/29/2019	Drake Maverick			
SMACKDOWN – 10/4/2019	Kofi Kingston			
NXT TAKEOVER XXV	Matt Riddle			
WRESTLEMANIA 33	Naomi (Standard - Black & Green)			
BACKLASH 2017	Naomi (Chase - Pink & Green)			
SUMMERSLAM 2019	Randy Orton			
SMACKDOWN – 1/29/2019	R-Truth			
1987	"Superstar" Billy Graham (Target)			

WWE ELITE COLLECTION SERIES 79 (2020)		MIB	LOOSE	VALUE
SMACKDOWN – 10/11/2019	Big E			
NXT TAKEOVER WAR GAMES '18	Bobby Fish (Standard - Snow Camo)			
WORLDS COLLIDE 2019	Bobby Fish (Chase - Black Trunks)			
MONEY IN THE BANK 2019	Daniel Bryan			
NXT TAKEOVER TORONTO 2019	Io Shirai			
SMACKDOWN – 9/24/2019	Roman Reigns			
EXTREME RULES 2019	The Undertaker (Walmart)			
SMACKDOWN – 10/11/2019	Xavier Woods			

WWE ELITE COLLECTION SERIES 80 (2020)		MIB	LOOSE	VALUE
SMACKDOWN – 10/11/2019	Bayley			
RAW – 5/6/2019	Erik			
RAW – 5/6/2019	Ivar			
SMACKDOWN – 10/4/2019	Kevin Owens			
NXT TAKEOVER WAR GAMES 2018	Kyle O'Reilly (Standard - Snow Camo)			
NXT TAKEOVER TORONTO 2019	Kyle O'Reilly (Chase - Black Trunks)			
RAW – 8/12/2019	Ricochet			
1983	Rocky Johnson (Target)			

WWE ELITE COLLECTION SERIES 81 (2021)

		MIB	LOOSE	VALUE
RAW – 7/1/2019	Angelo Dawkins			
NXT TAKEOVER PHOENIX	Bianca Belair			
RAW – 10/11/1999	Mae Young (Walmart)			
RAW – 7/1/2019	Montez Ford			
SURVIVOR SERIES 2019	Shinsuke Nakamura (Standard - Blue Suit)			
SMACKDOWN – 11/22/2019	Shinsuke Nakamura (Chase - Black Suit)			
SLAMBOREE 1993	"Stunning" Steve Austin			
SMACKDOWN – 10/4/2019	The Rock			

WWE ELITE COLLECTION SERIES 82 (2021)

		MIB	LOOSE	VALUE
HELL IN A CELL 2019	Alexa Bliss			
SURVIVOR SERIES 1987	Davey Boy Smith (Target)			
NXT WORLDS COLLIDE 2020	Finn Bálor			
SUMMERSLAM 1993	Jerry "The King" Lawler			
ROYAL RUMBLE 2020	John Morrison			
NXT – 1/22/2020	Keith Lee (Standard - Black Gear)			
NXT – 1/8/2020	Keith Lee (Chase - White Gear)			
WRESTLEMANIA 36	Rob Gronkowski			

WWE ELITE COLLECTION SERIES 83 (2021)

		MIB	LOOSE	VALUE
WRESTLEMANIA 36	Drew McIntyre			
SNME – 11/13/1990	Dusty Rhodes			
WRESTLEMANIA 36	Edge (Standard - Grey Tights)			
RAW – 1/27/2020	Edge (Chase - Black Tights)			
ROYAL RUMBLE 2020	King Corbin			
WCCW – 5/11/1985	Michael P.S. Hayes (Walmart)			
RAW – 8/26/2019	Sasha Banks			

WWE ELITE COLLECTION SERIES 84 (2021)		MIB	LOOSE	VALUE
205 LIVE – 10/24/2019	Angel Garza			
SMACKDOWN – 3/5/2019	Jeff Hardy (Standard - Blue Face Paint)			
ROYAL RUMBLE 2019	Jeff Hardy (Chase - Red Face Paint)			
RAW – 4/27/2020	Murphy			
NXT – 1/8/2020	Rhea Ripley			
CLASH 2019/SUMMERSLAM 2020	Roman Reigns			
SMACKDOWN – 1/3/2020	Sheamus			
RAW – 11/4/2019	Zelina Vega (Target)			

WWE ELITE COLLECTION SERIES 85 (2021)		MIB	LOOSE	VALUE
WRESTLEMANIA 36	Aleister Black (Standard - All Black Gear)			
WRESTLEMANIA 35	Aleister Black (Chase - White On Knee Pad)			
WRESTLEMANIA 36	Becky Lynch			
RAW – 6/10/2019	Bray Wyatt			
SUMMERSLAM 1995	Kama (Walmart)			
NXT – 5/6/2020	Karrion Kross			
ROYAL RUMBLE 2020	Liv Morgan			
WRESTLEMANIA 36	The Undertaker			

WWE ELITE COLLECTION SERIES 86 - SUMMERSLAM (2021)		MIB	LOOSE	VALUE
SUMMERSLAM 2018	Carmella			
SUMMERSLAM 1991	Colonel Mustafa (Target)			
SUMMERSLAM 2020	Seth Rollins			
SS 1991/CLASH XII	Sid Justice			
SUMMERSLAM 2020	"The Fiend" Bray Wyatt			
SUMMERSLAM 2018	The Miz			
SUMMERSLAM 1998	Triple H (Standard - Purple Tights)			
RAW – 1/11/1999	Triple H (Chase - Red Tights)			

WWE ELITE COLLECTION SERIES 87 (2021)		MIB	LOOSE	VALUE
PAYBACK 2020	Apollo Crews (Standard - Blue)			
SUMMERSLAM 2020	Apollo Crews (Chase - White Trunks)			
WRESTLEMANIA 36	Asuka			
SUMMERSLAM 2020	Braun Strowman			
NXT TAKEOVER: IN YOUR HOUSE 2020	Candice Lerae			
SMACKDOWN – 8/28/2020	Otis			
NXT – 6/24/2020	Santos Escobar			
WRESTLEMANIA V	Warlord (Walmart)			

WWE ELITE COLLECTION SERIES 88 (2021)		MIB	LOOSE	VALUE
NXT – 5/1/2019	Kushida			
EXTREME RULES 2020	MVP			
PAYBACK 2020	Rey Mysterio			
NXT TAKEOVER PORTLAND	Riddle			
HELL IN A CELL 2020	Roman Reigns			
SURVIVOR SERIES 2001	Trish Stratus (Standard - Pink Hat)			
WRESTLEMANIA X8	Trish Stratus (Chase - White Hat)			
WCW SATURDAY NIGHT – 9/9/1995	Zodiac (Target)			

WWE ELITE COLLECTION SERIES 89 (2022)		MIB	LOOSE	VALUE
SURVIVOR SERIES 2020	Bobby Lashley			
NXT TAKEOVER 31	Damian Priest			
RAW – 9/7/2020	Dominik Mysterio			
SURVIVOR SERIES 2020	Drew McIntyre			
MONEY IN THE BANK 2020	Nia Jax (Standard - Red Suit)			
BACKLASH 2020	Nia Jax (Chase - Purple Suit)			
SUMMERSLAM 1991	Sgt. Slaughter			
SUPERSTARS – 7/20/1995	The Goon (Walmart)			

WWE ELITE COLLECTION SERIES 90 (2022)		MIB	LOOSE	VALUE
SUPERSTARS – 7/18/1992	Big Boss Man (Standard - Blue Shirt)			
WCW STARRCADE 1992	Big Boss Man (Chase - The Boss)			
NXT TAKEOVER XXX	Bronson Reed			
	Chief Jay Strongbow (Target - **CANCELED**)			
HELL IN A CELL 2020	Jey Uso			
RAW – 10/19/2020	Mustafa Ali			
WRESTLEMANIA 37	Randy Orton			
RAW – 11/30/2020	Reckoning			

WWE ELITE COLLECTION SERIES 91 (2022)		MIB	LOOSE	VALUE
NXT – 3/17/2021	Austin Theory			
ROYAL RUMBLE 2021	Bianca Bel Air			
SUMMERSLAM 2005	Hulk Hogan			
ROYAL RUMBLE 2021	Kevin Owens			
ECW GUILTY AS CHARGEd '01	Rob Van Dam (Standard - Tiger Stripes)			
	Rob Van Dam (Chase - Rising Sun - **CANCELED**)			
SMACKDOWN – 12/25/2020	Sami Zayn			

WWE ELITE COLLECTION SERIES 92 (2022)		MIB	LOOSE	VALUE
NXT STAND & DELIVER 2021	Adam Cole (Standard - Green Trunks)			
NXT TAKEOVER WAR GAMES '18	Adam Cole (Chase - Snow Camo Trunks)			
ROYAL RUMBLE 2021	Charlotte Flair			
FASTLANE 2021	"The Fiend" Bray Wyatt			
SMACKDOWN – 2/12/2021	Rey Mysterio			
CLASH OF CHAMPIONS XXXII	Ric Flair			
NXT - 12/9/2020	Scarlett			

WWE ELITE COLLECTION SERIES 93 (2022)		MIB	LOOSE	VALUE
WRESTLEMANIA 37	Cesaro			
TAKEOVER: STAND & DELIVER '21	Karrion Kross			
TAKEOVER: STAND & DELIVER '21	Raquel Gonzalez			
WCW FALL BRAWL 1993	Ricky Steamboat (Standard - White Tights)			
WCW SPRING STAMPEDE 1994	Ricky Steamboat (Chase - Yellow Tights)			
WRESTLEMANIA 37	Seth Rollins			
RAW – 10/19/2020	T-Barr			

WWE ELITE COLLECTION SERIES 94 (2022)		MIB	LOOSE	VALUE
SUMMERSLAM 1992	Bret "Hitman" Hart (Standard - Pink Tights)			
SUMMERSLAM 1991	Bret "Hitman" Hart (Chase - Black Tights)			
SUMMERSLAM 1992	British Bulldog (Walmart)			
WRESTLEMANIA 37	Edge			
RAW – 10/19/2020	Mace			
TAKEOVER: STAND & DELIVER	Nash Carter			
RAW – 8/21/2000	Stephanie McMahon-Helmsley			
TAKEOVER- STAND & DELIVER	Wes Lee			

WWE ELITE COLLECTION SERIES 95 (2022)		MIB	LOOSE	VALUE
RAW – 9/12/2021	Big E			
SUMMERSLAM 2021	Bobby Lashley			
SMACKDOWN – 1/30/2003	Eddie Guerrero (Standard - Green Tights)			
SMACKDOWN – 1/2/2003	Eddie Guerrero (Chase - Black Tights)			
MONEY IN THE BANK 2021	Jimmy Uso			
MONEY IN THE BANK 2021	John Cena			
TAKEOVER: VENGEANCE DAY	Shotzi Blackheart			

WWE ELITE COLLECTION SERIES 96 (2022)		MIB	LOOSE	VALUE
CROWN JEWEL 2021	Brock Lesnar			
RAW – 6/14/2021	Doudrop (Standard - Blue Gear)			
SUMMERSLAM 2021	Doudrop (Chase - Green Gear)			
WRESTLING CHALLENGE – 9/4/1988	Hulk Hogan			
NXT – 8/10/2021	Ilja Dragunov			
MONEY IN THE BANK 2021	Kofi Kingston			
MONEY IN THE BANK 2021	Shinsuke Nakamura			

WWE ELITE COLLECTION SERIES 97 (2023)		MIB	LOOSE	VALUE
SUMMERSLAM 2021	Alexa Bliss			
RAW – 12/29/1997	Chainsaw Charlie			
MONEY IN THE BANK 2021	Omos			
ROYAL RUMBLE 2022	Ronda Rousey			
RAW – 7/21/2021	Sheamus			
SMACKDOWN – 10/29/2021	Xavier Woods (Standard - White Tights)			
RAW – 10/20/2021	Xavier Woods (Chase – He-Man Tights)			

WWE ELITE COLLECTION SERIES 98 (2023)		MIB	LOOSE	VALUE
DAY 1 – 1/1/2022	Big E			
RAW – 8/5/1996 & 9/16/1996	Faarooq Asaad			
EXTREME RULES 2021	Finn Bálor			
NXT HALLOWEEN HAVOC 2021	Mandy Rose			
SUMMERSLAM 2021	Randy Orton			
SMACKDOWN – 8/27/2021	Rick Boogs (Standard - Overalls Singlet)			
ROYAL RUMBLE 2022	Rick Boogs (Chase - Red Singlet)			

WWE ELITE COLLECTION SERIES 99 (2023)

		MIB	LOOSE	VALUE
ECW – 12/30/2008	Boogeyman (Standard - Red & Yellow Paint)			
ECW – 8/7/2007	Boogeyman (Chase - All Red Paint)			
SMACKDOWN – 12/10/2021	Brock Lesnar (Standard - Brown Overalls)			
SMACKDOWN – 12/17/2021	Brock Lesnar (Chase - Blue Overalls)			
SMACKDOWN 11/26/2021	Happy Corbin			
RAW – 12/6/2021	Queen Zelina			
CROWN JEWEL 2021	Matt Riddle			
RAW – 10/25/2021	Seth Rollins			

WWE ELITE COLLECTION SERIES 100 (2023)

		MIB	LOOSE	VALUE
SUPERSTARS – 2/7/1987	Andre The Giant (Standard - Checkered Jacket)			
SUPERSTARS – 3/21/1987	Andre The Giant (Chase - Blue Jacket)			
EXTREME RULES 2021	Becky Lynch			
SMACKDOWN – 4/15/2005	John Cena			
BASH AT THE BEACH 1998	Rey Mysterio			
ROYAL RUMBLE 2001	The Rock			
HALLOWEEN HAVOC 1991	"Stunning" Steve Austin			

WWE ELITE COLLECTION SERIES 101 (2023)

		MIB	LOOSE	VALUE
RAW – 4/18/2022	Cody Rhodes			
WRESTLEMANIA 38	Johnny Knoxville			
RAW 3/21/2022 & WM 38	Kevin Owens			
SMACKDOWN – 5/1/2003	Mr. America (Standard - Star Mask)			
SMACKDOWN – 6/26/2003	Mr. America (Chase - Stars & Stripes Mask)			
SMACKDOWN – 3/3/2022	Ricochet			
SMACKDOWN – 12/10/2021	Sonya Deville			

WWE ELITE COLLECTION SERIES 102 (2023)		MIB	LOOSE	VALUE
HELL IN A CELL 2022	Austin Theory (Standard - America Gear)			
WRESTLEMANIA 38	Austin Theory (Chase - Black Gear)			
RAW – 6/26/2000	Commissioner Foley			
HELL IN A CELL 2022	Edge			
SMACKDOWN – 4/8/2022	Gunther			
HELL IN A CELL 2022	Rhea Ripley			
WRESTLEMANIA 38	Sami Zayn			

WWE ELITE COLLECTION SERIES 103 (2023)		MIB	LOOSE	VALUE
RAW – 7/4/2022	Angelo Dawkins			
SUMMERSLAM 2022	Bobby Lashley			
MONEY IN THE BANK 2022	Liv Morgan			
SMACKDOWN – 7/1/2022	Montez Ford			
WRESTLEMANIA 38	Roman Reigns			
WRESTLEMANIA 32	Stardust (Standard - Polka Dots)			
RAW – 7/13/2015	Stardust (Chase - Blue Star Suit)			

WWE ELITE COLLECTION SERIES 104 (2023)		MIB	LOOSE	VALUE
RAW – 8/22/2022	AJ Styles			
NXT SPRING BREAKIN' 2022	Bron Breakker (Standard - Pink Singlet)			
NXT HALLOWEEN HAVOC 2022	Bron Breakker (Chase - Yellow Singlet)			
RAW – 9/12/2022	Dakota Kai			
CLASH AT THE CASTLE	Drew McIntyre			
NITRO – 7/5/1999	Rick Steiner			
SMACKDOWN – 9/9/2022	Solo Sikoa			

WWE ELITE COLLECTION SERIES 105 (2024)		MIB	LOOSE	VALUE
SMACKDOWN – 10/14/2022	Braun Strowman			
NXT 2.0 – 3/1/2022	Carmelo Hayes (Standard – Purple Shorts)			
NXT 2.0: VENGEANCE DAY 2022	Carmelo Hayes (Chase – Pink Shorts)			
RAW – 9/12/2022	Dominik Mysterio			
SMACKDWON – 10/14/2022	Iyo Sky			
RAW – 9/12/2022	Johnny Gargano			
BAD BLOOD 2003	Scott Steiner			

WWE ELITE COLLECTION SERIES 106 (2024)		MIB	LOOSE	VALUE
RAW – 3/27/2023	Chad Gable			
SURVIVOR SERIES 2022	Jey Uso			
SURVIVOR SERIES 2022	Jimmy Uso			
SUMMERSLAM 1994	Paul Bearer (Standard - Black Suit)			
RAW – 6/26/1998	Paul Bearer (Chase - Blue Suit)			
NXT – 12/13/2022	Roxanne Perez			
RAW – 3/6/2023	Sami Zayn			

WWE ELITE COLLECTION SERIES 107 (2024)		MIB	LOOSE	VALUE
NXT – 5/16/2023	Cora Jade			
SURVIVOR SERIES 2022	Finn Bálor			
NXT DEADLINE 2022	Grayson Waller (Standard - White Gear)			
NXT STAND & DELIVER 2023	Grayson Waller (Chase - Black Gear)			
RAW – 4/10/2023	Otis			
SURVIVOR SERIES 2022	Solo Sikoa			
RAW XXX	The Undertaker			

WWE ELITE COLLECTION SERIES 108 (2024)		MIB	LOOSE	VALUE
SUMMERSLAM 2022	Brock Lesnar			
BACKLASH 2023	Bronson Reed			
RAW – 3/27/2023	Chelsea Green (Standard - Blue Gear)			
ROYAL RUMBLE 2023	Chelsea Green (Chase - Orange Gear)			
TRIBUTE TO THE TROOPS 2022	LA Knight			
WRESTLEMANIA 39	Omos			
IWA 1995 & BURIED ALIVE 1996	Terry "Bam Bam" Gordy/The Executioner			

WWE ELITE COLLECTION SERIES 109 (2024)		MIB	LOOSE	VALUE
SMACKDOWN – 6/9/2023	Bayley			
RAW – 7/24/2023	Cody Rhodes			
ELIMINATION CHAMBER 2023	Damien Priest			
RAW – 1/9/2023	Dominik Mysterio			
MONEY IN THE BANK 2023	Seth Freakin' Rollins			
RAW – 8/7/2023	Shinsuke Nakamura (Standard – Black/White)			
PRO WRESTLING NOAH 1/1/24	Shinsuke Nakamura (Chase – Black/Red)			

WWE ELITE COLLECTION SERIES 110 (2024)		MIB	LOOSE	VALUE
BACKLASH 2023	Austin Theory			
WWWF 1970	Bruno Sammartino			
MONEY IN THE BANK 2023	Butch (Standard – White Singlet)			
SMACKDOWN – 6/9/2023	Butch (Chase – Green Singlet)			
SMACKDOWN – 6/2/2023	Elton Prince			
SMACKDOWN – 6/2/2023	Kit Wilson			
BACKLASH 2023	Rhea Ripley			
SUMMERSLAM 2023	Roman Reigns			

WWE ELITE COLLECTION SERIES 111 (2024)		MIB	LOOSE	VALUE
SUMMERSLAM 2023	Cody Rhodes			
SUMMERSLAM 2023	Finn Bálor			
SUMMERSLAM 2023	Ricochet			
ECW – 7/22/1997	Sandman (Standard – Black & White)			
ECW 3 WAY DANCE	Sandman (Chase – Red, White & Blue)			
NXT – 8/1/2023	Tony D'Angelo			
MONEY IN THE BANK 2023	Trish Stratus			

WWE ELITE COLLECTION SERIES 112 (2024)		MIB	LOOSE	VALUE
MONEY IN THE BANK 2023	Becky Lynch (Standard – Green & Yellow)			
PAYBACK 2023	Becky Lynch (Chase – Black & White)			
RAW – 3/19/2018	Bray Wyatt			
NXT – 8/1/2023	Channing "Stacks" Lorenzo			
RAW – 9/4/2023	JD McDonough			
PAYBACK 2023	Seth Freakin' Rollins			
RAW – 8/7/2023	Xavier Woods			

WWE ELITE COLLECTION SERIES 113 (2024)		MIB	LOOSE	VALUE
SMACKDOWN – 10/27/2023	Carlito (Standard – White Gear)			
SMACKDOWN – 11/10/2023	Carlito (Chase – Purple Gear)			
RAW – 5/23/2011	CM Punk (Standard – Macho Man Gear)			
GREAT AMERICAN BASH 2023	Dragon Lee			
RAW – 8/7/2023	Kofi Kingston			
GREAT AMERICAN BASH 2023	Tiffany Stratton			
NXT: NO MERCY 2023	Trick Williams			

WWE ELITE COLLECTION SERIES 114 (2024)		MIB	LOOSE	VALUE
NXT NO MERCY 2023	Bron Breakker			
NXT HEATWAVE – 8/22/2023	Ilja Dragunov			
RAW – 2/12/2024	Jey Uso (Standard – Black Pants)			
FASTLANE 2023	Jey Uso (Chase – Blue Pants)			
SMACKDOWN – 9/8/2023	Jimmy Uso (Standard – Black Pants)			
SMACKDOWN – 10/27/2023	Jimmy Uso (Chase – Red Pants)			
RAW – 1/15/2024	Tommaso Ciampa			
NXT STAND & DELIVER 2023	Zoey Stark			

WWE ELITE COLLECTION SERIES 115 (2025)		MIB	LOOSE	VALUE
ROYAL RUMBLE 2024	CM Punk			
RAW – 1/29/2024	Drew McIntyre (Standard – Black)			
WRESTLEMANIA 39	Drew McIntyre (Chase - White)			
SMACKDOWN – 3/1/2024	Kairi Sane			
RAW DAY 1 2024	R-Truth			
SMACKDOWN – 2/16/2024	The Rock			
SMACKDOWN – 1/19/2024	Tyler Bate			

WWE ELITE COLLECTION SERIES 116 (2025)		MIB	LOOSE	VALUE
SMACKDOWN – 12/22/2023	AJ Styles			
WCW SLAMBOREE 1993	Brian Pillman			
ROYAL RUMBLE 2024	Jade Cargill			
WRESTLEMANIA XL	Kevin Owens			
NXT – 1/9/2024	Lexis King			
SUVIVOR SERIES 2023	Randy Orton (Standard – Black on Black)			
WRESTLEMANIA XL	Randy Orton (Chase – Black & Gold)			

WWE ELITE COLLECTION SERIES 117 (2025)		MIB	LOOSE	VALUE
NXT STAND & DELIVER 2024	Axiom (Standard – Blue)			
NXT LEVEL UP -10/13/2023	Axiom (Chase – Pink)			
WRESTLEMANIA XL	Grayson Waller			
ROYAL RUMBLE 2024	Naomi			
ELIMINATION CHAMBER 2024	Rhea Ripley			
SMACKDOWN – 3/22/2024	Roman Reigns			
WRESTLEMANIA XL	Seth Freakin' Rollins			

WWE ELITE COLLECTION SERIES 118 (2025)		MIB	LOOSE	VALUE
SMACKDOWN – 6/28/2024	Jacob Fatu			
WRESTLEMANIA 22	John Cena (Collector's Edition)			
SMACKDOWN – 5/17/2024	Nia Jax (Standard – White)			
SMACKDOWN – 5/10/2024	Nia Jax (Chase – Red)			
SMACKDOWN – 5/17/2024	Solo Sikoa			
BACKLASH 2024	Tama Tonga			
SMACKDOWN – 5/31/2024	Tonga Loa			

WWE ELITE COLLECTION SERIES 119 (2025)		MIB	LOOSE	VALUE
SUMMERSLAM 2024	Bron Breakker			
RAW – 7/8/2024	"Dirty" Dominik Mysterio			
RAW – 6/17/2024	Dexter Lumis			
NXT HEATWAVE 2024	Ethan Page (Standard – Black & Gold)			
NXT NO MERCY 2024	Ethan Page (Chase – Black & Red)			
RAW ON NETFLIX DEBUT	John Cena (Collector's Edition)			
RAW – 7/8/2024	Liv Morgan			

WWE ELITE COLLECTION SERIES 120 (2025)		MIB	LOOSE	VALUE
SMACKDOWN – 6/28/2024	Cody Rhodes (Standard – Brown Suit)			
	Cody Rhodes (Chase – Pink Suit)			
	Joe Gacy			
RAW – 3/17/2025	John Cena (Collector's Edition)			
SUMMERSLAM 2024	LA Knight			
	Lola Vice			
SUMMERSLAM 2024	Roman Reigns			

WWE ELITE COLLECTION SERIES 121 (2025)		MIB	LOOSE	VALUE
	Alba Fyre			
	Austin Theory			
	Carmelo Hayes			
	CM Punk (Standard -)			
	CM Punk (Chase -)			
	John Cena			
	Oba Femi			

WWE ELITE COLLECTION SERIES 122 (2025)		MIB	LOOSE	VALUE

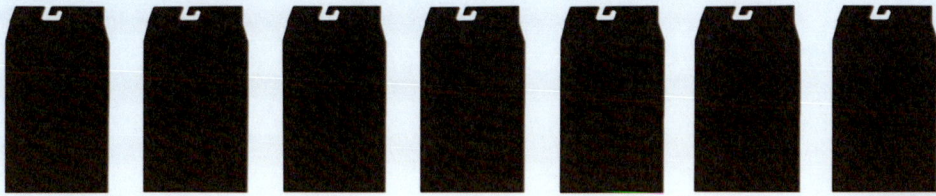

WWE ELITE COLLECTION SERIES 123 (2026)		MIB	LOOSE	VALUE

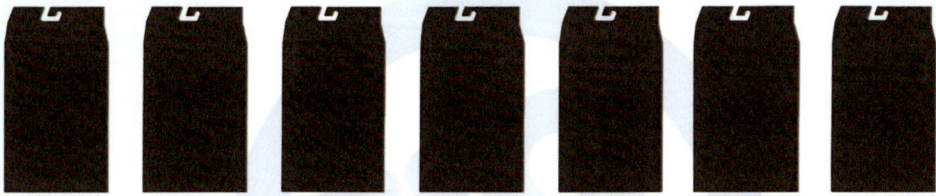

WWE ELITE COLLECTION SERIES 124 (2026)		MIB	LOOSE	VALUE

WWE ELITE COLLECTION SERIES 125 (2026)		MIB	LOOSE	VALUE

2010 WRESTLEMANIA 26 (TOYS 'R' US)	MIB	LOOSE	VALUE
Jack Swagger			
Rey Mysterio			
Triple H			
The Undertaker			

2011 WRESTLEMANIA 27 (TOYS 'R' US)	MIB	LOOSE	VALUE
Kofi Kingston			
Stone Cold Steve Austin			
The Miz			
The Rock			
The Undertaker			

2012 BEST OF PAY-PER-VIEW (TOYS 'R' US)		MIB	LOOSE	VALUE
SUMMERSLAM 2010	Bret "Hit Man" Hart			
SUMMERSLAM 2010	Daniel Bryan			
WRESTLEMANIA 27	John Cena			
WRESTLEMANIA 27	Triple H			
BUILD-A-FIGURE	Michael Cole			

2012 WRESTLEMANIA 28 (TOYS 'R' US)		MIB	LOOSE	VALUE
WRESTLEMANIA 28	Big Show			
WRESTLEMANIA 28	CM Punk			
WRESTLEMANIA 28	Shawn Michaels			
WRESTLEMANIA 28	The Miz			
BUILD-A-FIGURE	Ricardo Rodriguez			

2013 BEST OF PAY-PER-VIEW (TOYS 'R' US)		MIB	LOOSE	VALUE
NO WAY OUT	Christian			
EXTREME RULES	John Cena			
MONEY IN THE BANK	Sheamus			
NO WAY OUT	Sin Cara			
BUILD-A-FIGURE	John Laurinaitis			

2013 WRESTLEMANIA 29 (TOYS 'R' US)		MIB	LOOSE	VALUE
WRESTLEMANIA 29	Brock Lesnar			
WRESTLEMANIA 29	CM Punk			
WRESTLEMANIA 29	Daniel Bryan			
WRESTLEMANIA 29	John Cena			
BUILD-A-FIGURE	Paul Heyman			

2014 WRESTLEMANIA 30		MIB	LOOSE	VALUE
WRESTLEMANIA 10	Bret "Hit Man" Hart			
WRESTLEMANIA 14	Shawn Michaels			

2014 BEST OF PAY-PER-VIEW (TOYS 'R' US)		MIB	LOOSE	VALUE
PAYBACK	Alberto Del Rio			
MONEY IN THE BANK	CM Punk			
PAYBACK	Curtis Axel			
MONEY IN THE BANK	Randy Orton			
BUILD-A-FIGURE	Jim Ross			

2014 WRESTLEMANIA XXX (TOYS 'R' US)		MIB	LOOSE	VALUE
WRESTLEMANIA 30	Bray Wyatt			
WRESTLEMANIA 30	Daniel Bryan			
WRESTLEMANIA 30	John Cena			
WRESTLEMANIA 30	The Undertaker			
BUILD-A-FIGURE	Corporate Kane			

2015 WRESTLEMANIA 31		MIB	LOOSE	VALUE
WRESTLEMANIA 16	Kane			
WRESTLEMANIA 7	The Undertaker			

2016 WRESTLEMANIA 32		MIB	LOOSE	VALUE
WRESTLEMANIA 20	Brock Lesnar			
WRESTLEMANIA 31	The Undertaker			

2017 WRESTLEMANIA 33		MIB	LOOSE	VALUE
WRESTLEMANIA 12	Shawn Michaels			
WRESTLEMANIA 32	Triple H			

2017 SUMMERSLAM		MIB	LOOSE	VALUE
SUMMERSLAM 2016	Finn Balor			
SUMMERSLAM 1999	Mankind			

2018 WRESTLEMANIA 34		MIB	LOOSE	VALUE
WRESTLEMANIA 9	Brutus "The Barber" Beefcake			
WRESTLEMANIA 23	John Cena			
WRESTLEMANIA 33	Kevin Owens			
WRESTLEMANIA 33	Randy Orton			

2018 SUMMERSLAM (WALMART)		MIB	LOOSE	VALUE
SUMMERSLAM 2017	Dean Ambrose			
SUMMERSLAM 1998	Edge			
SUMMERSLAM 2004	Matt Hardy			
SUMMERSLAM 2017	Seth Rollins			

2018 SURVIVOR SERIES (WALMART)		MIB	LOOSE	VALUE
SUMMERSLAM 2018	AJ Styles			
SUMMERSLAM 2018	Alexa Bliss			
SUMMERSLAM 2018	Bobby Roode			

2019 WRESTLEMANIA 35		MIB	LOOSE	VALUE
WRESTLEMANIA 32	Sasha Banks			
WRESTLEMANIA 18	Scott Hall			
WRESTLEMANIA 19	Triple H			
WRESTLEMANIA 33	The Undertaker			

2019 SURVIVOR SERIES (WALMART)		MIB	LOOSE	VALUE
SURVIVOR SERIES 2017	Alicia Fox			
SURVIVOR SERIES 1987	Don Muraco			
SURVIVOR SERIES 2006	Jeff Hardy			
SURVIVOR SERIES 2017	Shinsuke Nakamura			

2020 ROYAL RUMBLE (TARGET)		MIB	LOOSE	VALUE
ROYAL RUMBLE 2007	Bobby Lashley			
ROYAL RUMBLE 2006	Lita			
ROYAL RUMBLE 1991	"Macho King" Randy Savage			
ROYAL RUMBLE 2013	The Rock			

2020 WRESTLEMANIA 36		MIB	LOOSE	VALUE
WRESTLEMANIA 19	Booker T			
WRESTLEMANIA 35	Kofi Kingston			
WRESTLEMANIA 22	Mick Foley			
WRESTLEMANIA 34	"Woken" Matt Hardy			
BUILD-A-FIGURE	"Dangerous" Danny Davis			

2020 SURVIVOR SERIES		MIB	LOOSE	VALUE
SURVIVOR SERIES 2018	Drew McIntyre			
SURVIVOR SERIES 2007	John Morrison			
SURVIVOR SERIES 2001	Kane			
SURVIVOR SERIES 2018	Samoa Joe			

2021 ROYAL RUMBLE (TARGET)		MIB	LOOSE	VALUE
ROYAL RUMBLE 2002	Stone Cold Steve Austin			
GREATEST RUMBLE	Titus O'Neil			
ROYAL RUMBLE 1990	Ultimate Warrior			
ROYAL RUMBLE 2008	Umaga			

2021 WRESTLEMANIA 37		MIB	LOOSE	VALUE
WRESTLEMANIA 17	Chyna			
WRESTLEMANIA 22	Edge			
WRESTLEMANIA 36	Goldberg			
WRESTLEMANIA 9	Shawn Michaels			
BUILD-A-FIGURE	Paul Ellering			

2021 SURVIVOR SERIES		MIB	LOOSE	VALUE
SURVIVOR SERIES 2019	Bayley			
SURVIVOR SERIES 1996	Bret "Hit Man" Hart			
SURVIVOR SERIES 1989	Hulk Hogan			
SURVIVOR SERIES 2019	Keith Lee			

2022 ROYAL RUMBLE (TARGET)		MIB	LOOSE	VALUE
ROYAL RUMBLE 2020	Big E			
ROYAL RUMBLE 2020	Dakota Kai			
ROYAL RUMBLE 1990	Earthquake			
ROYAL RUMBLE 1993	Yokozuna			
BUILD-A-FIGURE	Jimmy Hart			

2022 WRESTLEMANIA 38		MIB	LOOSE	VALUE
WRESTLEMANIA 36	AJ Styles			
WRESTLEMANIA 26	Bret "Hit Man" Hart			
WRESTLEMANIA 26	Shawn Michaels			
WRESTLEMANIA 19	Stone Cold Steve Austin			
BUILD-A-FIGURE	Vince McMahon			

2022 SUMMERSLAM		MIB	LOOSE	VALUE
SUMMERSLAM 2005	Randy Orton			
SUMMERSLAM 2005	Rey Mysterio			
SUMMERSLAM 1992	Sensational Sherri			
SUMMERSLAM 2005	Shawn Michaels			
BUILD-A-FIGURE	Dominik Mysterio			

2022 SURVIVOR SERIES		MIB	LOOSE	VALUE
SURVIVOR SERIES 2020	AJ Styles			
SURVIVOR SERIES 2021	Becky Lynch			
SURVIVOR SERIES 2009	Drew McIntyre			
SURVIVOR SERIES 1990	Ultimate Warrior			
BUILD-A-FIGURE	Rick Rude			

2023 ROYAL RUMBLE (TARGET)		MIB	LOOSE	VALUE
ROYAL RUMBLE 2018	Brie Bella			
ROYAL RUMBLE 2021	Damian Priest			
ROYAL RUMBLE 2006	Rey Mysterio			
ROYAL RUMBLE 1996	Vader			
BUILD-A-FIGURE	Dok Hendrix			

2023 WRESTLEMANIA 39		MIB	LOOSE	VALUE
WRESTLEMANIA 6	Dusty Rhodes			
WRESTLEMANIA 18	"Hollywood" Hulk Hogan			
WRESTLEMANIA 6	"Macho King" Randy Savage			
WRESTLEMANIA 18	The Rock			
BUILD-A-FIGURE	"Mean" Gene Okerlund			

2023 SUMMERSLAM		MIB	LOOSE	VALUE
SUMMERSLAM 2019	Dolph Ziggler			
SUMMERSLAM 1991	Hulk Hogan			
SUMMERSLAM 2021	Jey Uso			
SUMMERSLAM 1989	Zeus			
BUILD-A-FIGURE	Mr. Perfect			

2023 SURVIVOR SERIES		MIB	LOOSE	VALUE
SURVIVOR SERIES 2021	Charlotte Flair			
SURVIVOR SERIES 1996	Jerry "The King" Lawler			
SURVIVOR SERIES 2021	Kevin Owens			
SURVIVOR SERIES 2002	Shawn Michaels			
BUILD-A-FIGURE	British Bulldog			

2024 ROYAL RUMBLE		MIB	LOOSE	VALUE
ROYAL RUMBLE 2005	Batista			
ROYAL RUMBLE 2022	Beth Phoenix			
ROYAL RUMBLE 2022	Brock Lesnar			
ROYAL RUMBLE 2022	Ridge Holland			
BUILD-A-FIGURE	Virgil			

2024 WRESTLEMANIA XL		MIB	LOOSE	VALUE
WRESTLEMANIA XXVII	John Cena			
WRESTLEMANIA 38	Pat McAfee			
SURVIVOR SERIES 2011	The Rock			
WRESTLEMANIA XXVII	Trish Stratus			
BUILD-A-FIGURE	Nicholas			

2024 SUMMERSLAM		MIB	LOOSE	VALUE
SUMMERSLAM 2004	Kane			
SUMMERSLAM 1993	Lex Luger			
SUMMERSLAM 2015	The Undertaker			
SUMMERSLAM 1998	X-Pac			
BUILD-A-FIGURE	John Cone			

2024 SURVIVOR SERIES		MIB	LOOSE	VALUE
SURVIVOR SERIES 1993	Bushwhacker Butch			
SURVIVOR SERIES 1993	Bushwhacker Luke			
SURVIVOR SERIES 2022	Kevin Owens			
SURVIVOR SERIES 2022	Sami Zayn			
BUILD-A-FIGURE	Adam Pearce			

2025 ROYAL RUMBLE		MIB	LOOSE	VALUE
ROYAL RUMBLE 2023	Cody Rhodes			
ROYAL RUMBLE 2011	Diesel			
ROYAL RUMBLE 1990	Hulk Hogan			
ROYAL RUMBLE 2002	The Hurricane (Mask Photo)			
ROYAL RUMBLE 2002	The Hurricane (Facepaint Photo)			
BUILD-A-FIGURE	The Great Khali (2010)			

2025 WRESTLEMANIA 41		MIB	LOOSE	VALUE
WRESTLEMANIA 39	Bianca Belair			
WRESTLEMANIA IV	Bret "Hit Man" Hart			
WRESTLEMANIA 30	Hulk Hogan			
WRESTLEMANIA 39	Seth Freakin' Rollins			
BUILD-A-FIGURE	Howard Finkel (Wrestlemania 6)			

2025 SUMMERSLAM		MIB	LOOSE	VALUE
SUMMERSLAM 2023	Charlotte Flair			
SUMMERSLAM 2023	Roman Reigns			
SUMMERSLAM 2002	Shawn Michaels			
SUMMERSLAM 2002	Triple H			
BUILD-A-FIGURE	William Regal			

2025 SURVIVOR SERIES		MIB	LOOSE	VALUE
SURVIVOR SERIES 1995	1-2-3 Kid			
SURVIVOR SERIES 1993	Bret "Hit Man" Hart			
SURVIVOR SERIES 2023	Cody Rhodes			
SURVIVOR SERIES 2023	JD McDonagh			
BUILD-A-FIGURE	Nick Aldis			

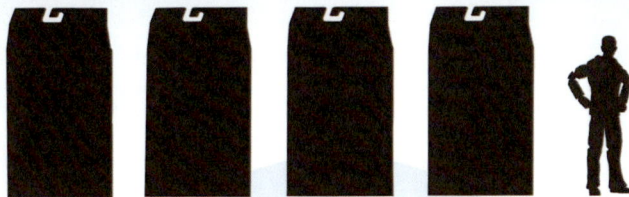

2026 ROYAL RUMBLE		MIB	LOOSE	VALUE
ROYAL RUMBLE				
ROYAL RUMBLE				
ROYAL RUMBLE				
ROYAL RUMBLE				
BUILD-A-FIGURE				

2026 WRESTLEMANIA 42		MIB	LOOSE	VALUE
WRESTLEMANIA				
WRESTLEMANIA				
WRESTLEMANIA				
WRESTLEMANIA				
BUILD-A-FIGURE				

2026 SUMMERSLAM		MIB	LOOSE	VALUE
SUMMERSLAM				
SUMMERSLAM				
SUMMERSLAM				
SUMMERSLAM				
BUILD-A-FIGURE				

BEST OF 2010		MIB	LOOSE	VALUE
ELITE SERIES 3	John Cena			
ELITE SERIES 4	Kane			
ELITE SERIES 2	Randy Orton			
ELITE SERIES 1	Rey Mysterio			
ELITE SERIES 2	Triple H			
ELITE SERIES 1	The Undertaker			

BEST OF 2011		MIB	LOOSE	VALUE
ELITE SERIES 11	John Cena			
ELITE SERIES 10	John Morrison			
ELITE SERIES 9	Randy Orton			
ELITE SERIES 11	Rey Mysterio			
ELITE SERIES 8	Sheamus			

TOP PICKS 2018	MIB	LOOSE	VALUE
AJ Styles			
Braun Strowman			
Finn Balor			
Seth Rollins			

TOP PICKS 2019	MIB	LOOSE	VALUE
AJ Styles			
Braun Strowman			
Finn Balor			
Seth Rollins			

STROWMAN RICOCHET REIGNS ROLLINS

TOP PICKS 2020	MIB	LOOSE	VALUE
Braun Strowman			
Ricochet			
Roman Reigns			
Seth Rollins			

McINTYRE KINGSTON REIGNS BRAY WYATT McINTYRE CENA MYSTERIO REIGNS

TOP PICKS 2021		MIB	LOOSE	VALUE
WAVE 1	Drew McIntyre			
	Kofi Kingston			
	Roman Reigns			
	"The Fiend" Bray Wyatt			
WAVE 2	Drew McIntyre			
	John Cena			
	Rey Mysterio			
	Roman Reigns			

WAVE 1 — GOLDBERG JEFF HARDY ROMAN REIGNS
WAVE 2 — REY MYSTERIO THE ROCK UNDERTAKER

WAVE 3 — DREW McINTYRE JOHN CENA RANDY ORTON REY MYSTERIO

TOP PICKS 2022		MIB	LOOSE	VALUE
WAVE 1	Goldberg			
	Jeff Hardy			
	Roman Reigns			
WAVE 2	Rey Mysterio			
	The Rock			
	The Undertaker			
WAVE 3	Drew McIntyre			
	John Cena			
	Randy Orton			
	Rey Mysterio			

TOP PICKS 2023		MIB	LOOSE	VALUE
WAVE 1	Rey Mysterio			
	Roman Reigns			
	Seth Rollins			
WAVE 2	Bobby Lashley			
	John Cena			
	Ronda Rousey			
WAVE 3	Jimmy Uso			
	Roman Reigns			
	The Rock			
WAVE 4	Cody Rhodes			
	Rey Mysterio			
	Riddle			

TOP PICKS 2024		MIB	LOOSE	VALUE
WAVE 1	John Cena			
	Roman Reigns			
	Seth Rollins			
WAVE 2	Cody Rhodes			
	Logan Paul			
	Sheamus			
WAVE 3	Gunther			
	Rey Mysterio			
	Roman Reigns			
WAVE 4	Cody Rhodes			
	The Rock			
	Solo Sikoa			

WAVE 1
WAVE 2
WAVE 3
WAVE 2
WAVE 4

TOP PICKS 2025		MIB	LOOSE	VALUE
WAVE 1	Jey Uso			
	Seth Rollins			
	Roman Reigns			
WAVE 2	CM Punk			
	Logan Paul			
	Stone Cold Steve Austin			
WAVE 2 (NETFLIX)	CM Punk			
	Logan Paul			
	Stone Cold Steve Austin			
WAVE 3	Damian Priest			
	"Dirty" Dominik Mysterio			
	LA Knight			
WAVE 4	Cody Rhodes			
	Rey Mysterio			
	Solo Sikoa			

LOST LEGENDS		MIB	LOOSE	VALUE
ELITE SERIES 20	Chris Jericho			
LEGENDS 2	Kamala			
	Magnum T.A.			
ELITE SERIES 19	Shawn Michaels			
LEGENDS 6	Ultimate Warrior			
ELITE SERIES 23	The Undertaker			

GREATEST HITS SERIES 1		MIB	LOOSE	VALUE
LEGENDS 5	Bam Bam Bigelow			
FLASHBACK 3	Jake "The Snake" Roberts			
ELITE 24	Rey Mysterio			
HALL OF CHAMPIONS 1	Rikishi			
BEST OF ATTITUDE ERA	The Rock			
ELITE 8	The Undertaker			

GREATEST HITS SERIES 2		MIB	LOOSE	VALUE
ELITE 33	Batista			
LEGENDS 10	Diamond Dallas Page			
FLASHBACK 3	King Harley Race			
ELITE WM 31	Seth Rollins			
ELITE WM XXX	Shawn Michaels			
HALL OF CHAMPIONS 1	The Undertaker			

GREATEST HITS SERIES 3		MIB	LOOSE	VALUE
LEGENDS 19	Brutus "The Barber" Beefcake			
THEN, NOW, FOREVER 2	Earthquake			
ELITE 10	R-Truth			
HOLLYWOOD SERIES 1	"Rowdy" Roddy Piper as John Nada			
ELITE 33	Seth Rollins			
HOLLYWOOD SERIES 2	The Rock as The Scorpion King			
THEN, NOW, FOREVER 2	Typhoon			

GREATEST HITS SERIES 4		MIB	LOOSE	VALUE
ELITE 74	AJ Styles			
SUVIVOR SERIES 2021	Hulk Hogan			
2020 ELITE 2-PACK	Rey Mysterio			
ELITE 90	Randy Orton			

GREATEST HITS SERIES 5		MIB	LOOSE	VALUE
ELITE 109	Dominik Mysterio			
ELITE 108	LA Knight			
ELITE 110	Roman Reigns			
ELITE 109	Seth Freakin' Rollins			

GREATEST HITS SERIES 6		MIB	LOOSE	VALUE
ELITE 13	Cody Rhodes			
ELITE 23	John Cena			
ELITE 13	King Sheamus			
WRESTLEMANIA XXVII	The Miz			
WOMEN'S DIVISION (UNRELEASED)	Natalya (Standard – Criss Cross Gear)			
	Natalya (Chase – Bedazzled Gear)			
ELITE 33	Roman Reigns			

GREATEST HITS SERIES 7		MIB	LOOSE	VALUE
ELITE 2	Batista			
HULKAMANIA 3-PACK	Hulk Hogan			
ELITE 31	Jey Uso			
ELITE 31	Jimmy Uso			
ELITE 21	Rey Mysterio			
HALL OF CHAMPIONS 2	Ron Simmons			
ELITE 25	Seth Rollins			
ELITE 27	The Undertaker			

GREATEST HITS SERIES 8		MIB	LOOSE	VALUE
ROYAL RUMBLE 2025	Cody Rhodes			
RINGSIDE EXCLUSIVE	Gunther			
COLLECTOR'S EDITION	John Cena			
ELITE 110	Roman Reigns			
ROYAL RUMBLE 2021	Stone Cold Steve Austin			

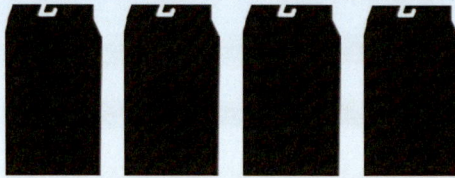

GREATEST HITS SERIES 9		MIB	LOOSE	VALUE
	Cody Rhodes			
	Jacob Fatu			
	Logan Paul			
	Stone Cold Steve Austin			

GREATEST HITS SERIES 10		MIB	LOOSE	VALUE

FROM THE VAULT SERIES 1 (RINGSIDE COLLECTIBLES)		MIB	LOOSE	VALUE
ELITE 45	Bubba Ray Dudley			
ELITE 45	D-Von Dudley			
DEFINING MOMENTS	John Cena			
RINGSIDE EXCLUSIVE	Kane			
ELITE 7	Shawn Michaels			
ELITE 7	Triple H			
HALL OF CHAMPIONS 3	Ultimate Warrior			
DEFINING MOMENTS	The Undertaker			

FROM THE VAULT SERIES 2 (RINGSIDE COLLECTIBLES)		MIB	LOOSE	VALUE
HALL OF CHAMPIONS 3	Billy Gunn			
ELITE 16	Diesel			
LEGENDS 6	Eddie Guerrero			
TRIBAL CHIEF VS. BEAST	Paul Heyman			
ELITE 27	Rikishi			
HALL OF CHAMPIONS 3	Road Dogg			
RINGSIDE EXCLUSIVE	Shawn Michaels			
RINGSIDE EXCLUSIVE	The Undertaker (as Kane)			

FROM THE VAULT SERIES 3 (RINGSIDE COLLECTIBLES)		MIB	LOOSE	VALUE
SES RINGSIDE EXCLUSIVE	CM Punk			
WM HOLLYWOOD	"Hollywood" Hulk Hogan			
DEFINING MOMENTS 1	Shawn Michaels			
FLASHBACK 1	Yokozuna (Standard – Black Tights)			
UNRELEASED	Yokozuna (Chase – White Tights)			

FROM THE VAULT SERIES 4 (RINGSIDE COLLECTIBLES)		MIB	LOOSE	VALUE
WRESTLEMANIA XXX	Bray Wyatt			
DEFINING MOMENTS	CM Punk (Stand Alone Release)			
DEFINING MOMENTS	Cody Rhodes			
LEGENDS 6	Razor Ramon			
DEFINING MOMENTS	Ultimate Warrior			

FROM THE VAULT SERIES 5 (RINGSIDE COLLECTIBLES)		MIB	LOOSE	VALUE
ELITE 48	The Boogeyman			
ELITE 7	Hornswoggle			
THE CHAMP IS HERE	John Cena			
SUMMERSLAM 2024	John Cone (Standard – Black & White)			
UNRELEASED	John Cone (Chase – Blue)			

FROM THE VAULT SERIES 6 (RINGSIDE COLLECTIBLES)		MIB	LOOSE	VALUE
RINGSIDE EXCLUSIVE	Cactus Jack			
RINGSIDE EXCLUSIVE	Kevin Nash			
UNRELEASED	Rob Van Dam			
RINGSIDE EXCLUSIVE	Scott Hall			

FROM THE VAULT SERIES 7 (RINGSIDE COLLECTIBLES)		MIB	LOOSE	VALUE

FROM THE VAULT SERIES 8 (RINGSIDE COLLECTIBLES)		MIB	LOOSE	VALUE

WAVE 1  WAVE 2  WAVE 3  WAVE 4  WAVE 5

DEFINING MOMENTS (ORIGINAL)		MIB	LOOSE	VALUE
WAVE 1	"Macho Man" Randy Savage			
	Shawn Michaels			
WAVE 2	The Rock			
	Ultimate Warrior			
WAVE 3	Ricky "The Dragon" Steamboat			
	Triple H			
WAVE 4	Stone Cold Steve Austin			
	The Undertaker			
WAVE 5	Bret "Hit Man" Hart			
	John Cena			

DEFINING MOMENTS ULTIMATE WARRIOR EXCLUSIVES			MIB	LOOSE	VALUE
ULTIMATE WARRIOR.COM	1 OF 15	Ultimate Warrior (One Warrior Nation)			
	1 OF 15	Ultimate Warrior (Granite)			
	1 OF 15	Ultimate Warrior (2K14 Commercia)			

DEFINING MOMENTS (REVIVAL)		MIB	LOOSE	VALUE
2014	Ric Flair			
2015	Hulk Hogan			
	Razor Ramon			
	Sting			
	The Undertaker			
2016	Stone Cold Steve Austin			
	Sting			
	Ultimate Warrior			
	John Cena			
2017	Ric Flair (Closed Robe)			
	Ric Flair (Open Robe)			
	Shinsuke Nakamura			
	"Macho Man" Randy Savage			
	Chris Jericho			

DEFINING MOMENTS RINGSIDE EXCLUSIVE 4-PACK SERIES 1		MIB	LOOSE	VALUE
	Bret "Hit Man" Hart			
	Cody Rhodes			
	Mankind			
	Shawn Michaels			

DEFINING MOMENTS RINGSIDE EXCLUSIVE 4-PACK SERIES 2		MIB	LOOSE	VALUE
	CM Punk			
	Kane			
	LA Knight			
	Rob Van Dam			

DEFINING MOMENTS RINGSIDE EXCLUSIVE 4-PACK SERIES 3	MIB	LOOSE	VALUE
Kurt Angle			
Logan Paul			
Paul Heyman			
Stone Cold Steve Austin			

2026 DEFINING MOMENTS (RINGSIDE EXCLUSIVE)	MIB	LOOSE	VALUE
CM Punk			
Jey Uso			
Penta			

HALL OF FAME SERIES 1 (TARGET)		MIB	LOOSE	VALUE
CLASS OF 2004	Sgt. Slaughter			
CLASS OF 2009	Stone Cold Steve Austin			
CLASS OF 2013	Trish Stratus			
CLASS OF 2014	Ultimate Warrior			

HALL OF FAME SERIES 2 (TARGET)		MIB	LOOSE	VALUE
CLASS OF 2006	Eddie Guerrero			
CLASS OF 2005	Hulk Hogan			
CLASS OF 2004	Tito Santana			
CLASS OF 2012	Yokozuna			

HALL OF FAME SERIES 3 (TARGET)		MIB	LOOSE	VALUE
CLASS OF 2013	Cactus Jack (Stop Release)			
CLASS OF 2015	"Macho King" Randy Savage			
CLASS OF 2010	"Million Dollar Man" Ted Dibiase			
CLASS OF 2005	"The Mouth Of The South" Jimmy Hart			

HALL OF FAME SERIES 4 (TARGET)		MIB	LOOSE	VALUE
CLASS OF 2012	Edge			
CLASS OF 2007	Jerry "The King" Lawler			
CLASS OF 2013	King Booker			
CLASS OF 2016	Sting			

HALL OF FAME SERIES 5 (TARGET)		MIB	LOOSE	VALUE
CLASS OF 2015	Diesel			
CLASS OF 1995	George "The Animal" Steele			
CLASS OF 2014	Jake "The Snake" Roberts			
CLASS OF 2005	"Rowdy" Roddy Piper			

HALL OF FAME 2-PACKS (TARGET)		MIB	LOOSE	VALUE
CLASS OF 2016	Papa Shango			
CLASS OF 2014	Ultimate Warrior			
CLASS OF 2007	Afa			
CLASS OF 2007	Sika			

HALL OF FAME - FOUR HORSEMEN (TARGET)		MIB	LOOSE	VALUE
CLASS OF 2012	Ric Flair			
CLASS OF 2012	Arn Anderson			
CLASS OF 2012	Barry Windham			
CLASS OF 2012	Tully Blanchard			

HALL OF FAME - HEENAN FAMILY (TARGET)		MIB	LOOSE	VALUE
CLASS OF 1993	Andre The Giant			
CLASS OF 2004	Bobby Heenan			
CLASS OF 2007	Mr. Perfect			
CLASS OF 2004	Big John Studd			

HALL OF FAME – NITRO NOTABLES (TARGET)		MIB	LOOSE	VALUE
CLASS OF 2006	Eddie Guerrero			
CLASS OF 2015	Kevin Nash			
CLASS OF 2014	Scott Hall			
CLASS OF 2015	Larry Zybysko			

NXT TAKEOVER SERIES 1 (TARGET)	MIB	LOOSE	VALUE
Austin Aries			
Bayley			
No Way Jose			
Seth Rollins			

NXT TAKEOVER SERIES 2 (TARGET)	MIB	LOOSE	VALUE
Asuka			
Dash Wilder			
Scott Dawson			
Shinsuke Nakamura			

NXT TAKEOVER SERIES 3 (TARGET)	MIB	LOOSE	VALUE
Alexander Rusev			
Bobby Roode			
Ember Moon			
Roman Reigns			

NXT TAKEOVER SERIES 4 (TARGET)	MIB	LOOSE	VALUE
Aleister Black			
Drew McIntyre			
Killian Dain			
Ruby Riott			

NXT TAKEOVER SERIES 5	MIB	LOOSE	VALUE
Andrade "Cien" Almas (Ringside Collectibles)			
Hideo Itami		CANCELLED	
Roderick Strong		CANCELLED	
Titus O'Neil		CANCELLED	

THEN, NOW, FOREVER SERIES 1 (WALMART)	MIB	LOOSE	VALUE
Bam Bam Bigelow			
Rusev			
The Rock			
Tyler Breeze			

THEN, NOW, FOREVER SERIES 2 (WALMART)	MIB	LOOSE	VALUE
Earthquake			
"Macho Man" Randy Savage			
Sami Zayn			
Typhoon			

THEN, NOW, FOREVER SERIES 3 (WALMART)	MIB	LOOSE	VALUE
Chad Gable			
Jason Jordan			
Miss Elizabeth			
Seth Rollins			

THEN, NOW, FOREVER 3-PACKS (WALMART)		MIB	LOOSE	VALUE
BASH AT THE BEACH	Lex Luger			
	"Macho Man" Randy Savage			
	Sting			
THE SHIELD	Seth Rollins			
	Dean Ambrose			
	Roman Reigns			

NETWORK SPOTLIGHT SERIES 1 (TOYS 'R' US)	MIB	LOOSE	VALUE
AJ Styles			
Bayley			
Big Boss Man			
Dean Ambrose			
Finn Balor			
Hunter Hearst Helmsley			
Mr. McMahon			
Roman Reigns			
Shawn Michaels			
The Ringmaster			
The Undertaker			
TJ Perkins			

NETWORK SPOTLIGHT SERIES 2 (TARGET)	MIB	LOOSE	VALUE
Asuka			
Diesel			
Jinder Mahal			
Rey Mysterio			

NETWORK SPOTLIGHT SERIES 3 (TARGET)	MIB	LOOSE	VALUE
Kurt Angle			
Ricochet			
Wendi Richter			
"Woken" Matt Hardy			

WOMEN'S DIVISION (WALGREENS)	MIB	LOOSE	VALUE
Sasha Banks			
Becky Lynch			
Maryse			
Alexa Bliss			
Paige		CANCELLED	

FLASHBACK SERIES 1 (WALMART)	MIB	LOOSE	VALUE
Mean Gene Okerlund			
Syxx			
Ultimate Warrior			
Yokozuna			

FLASHBACK SERIES 2 (WALMART)	MIB	LOOSE	VALUE
Alundra Blayze			
Doink The Clown			
Razor Ramon			
Shawn Michaels			

	FLASHBACK SERIES 3 (WALMART)	MIB	LOOSE	VALUE
	Jake "The Snake" Roberts			
	King Harley Race			
	Ricky "The Dragon" Steamboat			
	Stone Cold Steve Austin			
BUILD-A-FIGURE	Commissioner Shawn Michaels			

	HALL OF CHAMPIONS SERIES 1 (TARGET)	MIB	LOOSE	VALUE
2005	Batista			
1997	Eddie Guerrero			
2000	Rikishi			
1999	The Undertaker			

	HALL OF CHAMPIONS SERIES 2 (TARGET)	MIB	LOOSE	VALUE
2016	Johnny Gargano			
1998	Kane			
1992	Ron Simmons			
2016	Tommaso Ciampa			

HALL OF CHAMPIONS SERIES 3 (TARGET)		MIB	LOOSE	VALUE
1998	Billy Gunn			
1991	Paul Bearer			
1998	Road Dogg			
1990	Ultimate Warrior			

BEST OF ATTITUDE ERA (AMAZON)	MIB	LOOSE	VALUE
Chris Jericho			
Stone Cold Steve Austin			
The Rock			
Triple H			

RETROFEST (GAMESTOP)		MIB	LOOSE	VALUE
SERIES 1	"Macho Man" Randy Savage			
	Shawn Michaels			
SERIES 2	"Hacksaw" Jim Duggan			
	Honky Tonk Man			
	Ric Flair			

RETROFEST SERIES 3 (TARGET.COM)	MIB	LOOSE	VALUE
Iron Sheik			
Mr. Perfect			

FAN CENTRAL SERIES 1 (TOYS 'R' US)	MIB	LOOSE	VALUE
Big Show			
Bobby "The Brain" Heenan			
Mark Henry			
Triple H			

FAN CENTRAL SERIES 2 (WALMART)	MIB	LOOSE	VALUE
Akira Tozawa			
Carmella			
Daniel Bryan			
Mojo Rawley			

ENTRANCE GREATS		MIB	LOOSE	VALUE
SERIES 1	Jeff Hardy			
	Kurt Angle			
SERIES 2	Bobby Roode			
	Finn Balor			
SERIES 3	Elias			
	Goldberg			

GHOSTBUSTERS (WALMART)	MIB	LOOSE	VALUE
John Cena			
Shawn Michaels			
Stone Cold Steve Austin			
The Rock			
The Undertaker			

DECADE OF DOMINATION SERIES 1 (WALMART)	MIB	LOOSE	VALUE
John Cena			
Mark Henry			
Natalya			
Randy Orton			
The Undertaker			

DECADE OF DOMINATION SERIES 2 (WALMART)	MIB	LOOSE	VALUE
Beth Phoenix			
Big Show			
Kane (w/ Clean Shaven Alternate Head)			
Kane (w/ Goatee on Alternate Head)			
Kofi Kingston			
Triple H			

FAN TAKEOVER SERIES 1 (AMAZON)	MIB	LOOSE	VALUE
Adam Cole			
Ricky "The Dragon" Steamboat			
Seth Rollins			
Shayna Baszler			

FAN TAKEOVER SERIES 2 (AMAZON)	MIB	LOOSE	VALUE
Christian			
Johnny Gargano			
Randy Orton			
X-Pac			

HOLLYWOOD SERIES 1 (WALMART)	MIB	LOOSE	VALUE
John Cena as Jakob Toretto			
"Rowdy" Roddy Piper as John Nada			
The Rock as Luke Hobbs			

HOLLYWOOD SERIES 2 (WALMART)	MIB	LOOSE	VALUE
Andre The Giant as Bigfoot			
Roman Reigns as Matteo Hobbs			
The Rock as The Scorpion King			

RUTHLESS AGGRESSION SERIES 1 (WALMART)		MIB	LOOSE	VALUE
RA 2	Batista			
RA 1	Brock Lesnar			
RA 29	Shawn Michaels			

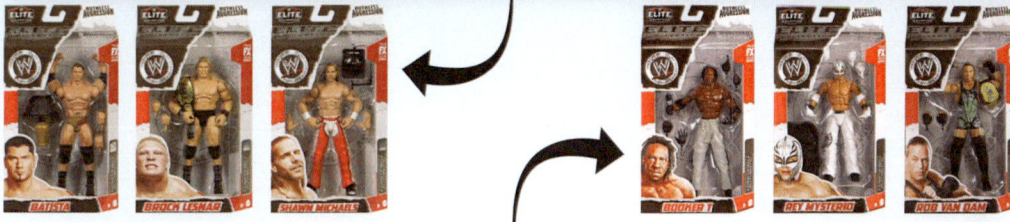

RUTHLESS AGGRESSION SERIES 2 (WALMART)		MIB	LOOSE	VALUE
RA 9	Booker T			
RA 1	Rey Mysterio			
RA 21	Rob Van Dam			

RUTHLESS AGGRESSION SERIES 3 (WALMART)		MIB	LOOSE	VALUE
RA 38	John Cena			
RA 5	Kevin Nash			
RA 13	Shelton Benjamin			

RUTHLESS AGGRESSION SERIES 4 (WALMART)		MIB	LOOSE	VALUE
RA 1/PPV 12	Eric Bischoff			
RA 9	Stone Cold Steve Austin			
RA 4	The Undertaker			

RUTHLESS AGGRESSION SERIES 5 (WALMART)		MIB	LOOSE	VALUE
RA 35.5	Edge			
PPV 10	JBL			
RA 4	Torrie Wilson			

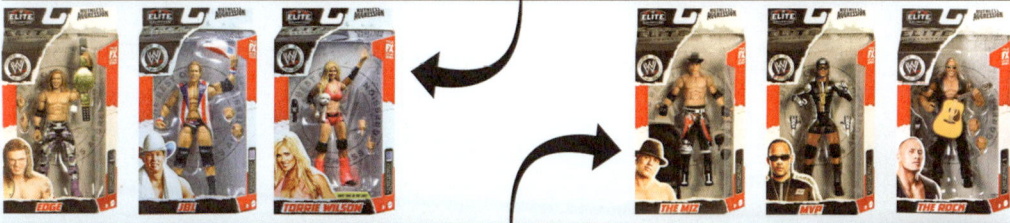

RUTHLESS AGGRESSION SERIES 6 (WALMART)		MIB	LOOSE	VALUE
RA 28	The Miz			
DA 14	MVP			
RA 4	The Rock			

MONDAY NIGHT WAR SERIES 1 (WALMART)		MIB	LOOSE	VALUE
NITRO	Hulk Hogan			
NITRO	Scott Hall			
RAW	Stone Cold Steve Austin			
RAW	The Undertaker			
BUILD-A-FIGURE	Lex Luger			

MONDAY NIGHT WAR SERIES 2 (WALMART)		MIB	LOOSE	VALUE
RAW	"Diesel"			
NITRO	Kevin Nash			
NITRO	Rey Mysterio Jr.			
RAW	Triple H			
BUILD-A-FIGURE	Teddy Long			

MONDAY NIGHT WAR SERIES 3 (WALMART)		MIB	LOOSE	VALUE
NITRO	Booker T (Standard – Black Gear)			
NITRO	Booker T (Chase – Blue Gear)			
RAW	Rob Van Dam			
NITRO	Stevie Ray (Standard – Black Gear)			
NITRO	Stevie Ray (Chase – Blue Gear)			
RAW	The Rock			
BUILD-A-FIGURE	The Disciple			

MONDAY NIGHT WAR SERIES 4 (WALMART)		MIB	LOOSE	VALUE
RAW – 10/12/98	Big Boss Man			
NITRO – 1/11/99	Curt Hennig			
NITRO – 12/8/97	Diamond Dallas Page (Standard – Light Jeans)			
NITRO	Diamond Dallas Page (Chase – Dark Jeans)			
RAW – 9/22/97	Stone Cold Steve Austin			
BUILD-A-FIGURE	Commissioner Michaels (Raw – 11/23/98)			

MONDAY NIGHT WAR SERIES 5 (WALMART)		MIB	LOOSE	VALUE
RAW – 8/21/00	Lita			
RAW – 12/18/95	Razor Ramon			
NITRO – 4/21/97	Syxx (Standard – No Logo Singlet)			
NITRO	Syxx (Chase – Thug Singlet)			
NITRO – 8/17/98	Ultimate Warrior			
BUILD-A-FIGURE	Dusty Rhodes (Nitro – 11/30/98)			

MONDAY NIGHT WAR SERIES 6 (WALMART)		MIB	LOOSE	VALUE
NITRO – 12/29/97	Booker T (Standard – Black Tights)			
NITRO	Booker T (Chase – White Tights)			
RAW – 9/25/95	British Bulldog			
NITRO – 2/1/99	Hardcore Hak			
RAW – 6/26/00	Kane			
BUILD-A-FIGURE	Golga (Raw – 9/12/98)			

MONDAY NIGHT WAR SERIES 7 (WALMART)		MIB	LOOSE	VALUE
RAW – 11/22/99	Albert			
NITRO – 7/22/97	The Great Muta (Standard – NWO Facepaint)			
NITRO	The Great Muta (Chase – Symbol Facepaint)			
NITRO – 11/9/98	"Hollywood" Hulk Hogan			
RAW – 5/19/98	Jerry "The King" Lawler			
BUILD-A-FIGURE	"Trillionaire" Ted Dibiase (Nitro – 10/28/96)			

MONDAY NIGHT WAR SERIES 8 (WALMART)		MIB	LOOSE	VALUE
RAW – 5/5/97	Brian Pillman			
NITRO – 4/10/00	Eric Bischoff			
NITRO – 5/27/96	The Shark (Standard – Shark Top)			
NITRO	The Shark (Chase – Blue Top)			
RAW – 5/22/00	Undertaker			
BUILD-A-FIGURE	Michael Cole			

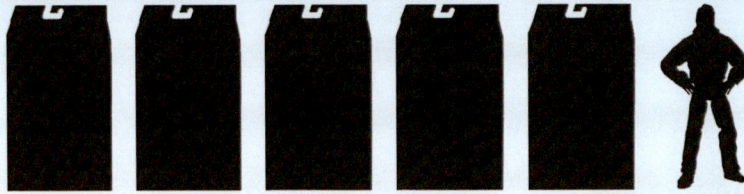

MONDAY NIGHT WAR SERIES 9 (WALMART)		MIB	LOOSE	VALUE
	Fatu			
	G.I. Bro			
	Guardian Angel			
	The Rock			
BUILD-A-FIGURE				

MONDAY NIGHT WAR GREATEST HITS SERIES 1 (WALMART)		MIB	LOOSE	VALUE
NITRO – 11/16/98	Bam Bam Bigelow			
NITRO – 1/6/97	Eddie Guerrero			
RAW – 3/30/98	Triple H			
RAW – 12/22/97	Shawn Michaels			
BUILD-A-FIGURE	Vincent (Nitro – 8/4/97)			

MONDAY NIGHT WAR GREATEST HITS SERIES 2 (WALMART)		MIB	LOOSE	VALUE
NITRO – 12/6/99	Bret "Hit Man" Hart			
NITRO – 8/4/97	Diamond Dallas Page (Standard – Purple Trimmed Pants)			
NITRO	Diamond Dallas Page (Chase – Blue Trimmed Pants)			
RAW – 6/30/97	Ken Shamrock			
RAW – 1/8/96	The Ringmaster			
BUILD-A-FIGURE	Gorilla Monsoon (Raw – 4/21/97)			

TEENAGE MUTANT NINJA TURTLES X WWE (TARGET)			MIB	LOOSE	VALUE
SERIES 1	MICHELANGELO	Kofi Kingston			
	SHREDDER	Roman Reigns			
	DONATELLO	Xavier Woods			
SERIES 2	CASEY JONES	Cody Rhodes			
	RAPHAEL	Rey Mysterio			
	LEONARDO	Seth Rollins			

2010-2012 RINGSIDE COLLECTIBLES EXCLUSIVES		MIB	LOOSE	VALUE
2010	Rey Mysterio			
2011	CM Punk			
	Kane			
2012	Bret "Hit Man" Hart			
	"Macho Man" Randy Savage			
	Stone Cold Steve Austin			

2013-2014 RINGSIDE COLLECTIBLES EXCLUSIVES		MIB	LOOSE	VALUE
2013	Brock Lesnar			
	Cactus Jack			
	Kane			
2014	CM Punk			
	Edge			
	The Rock			

2015-2016 RINGSIDE COLLECTIBLES EXCLUSIVES		MIB	LOOSE	VALUE
2015	Hulk Hogan			
	Scott Hall			
	Shawn Michaels			
2016	Kevin Nash			
	"Macho Man" Randy Savage			
	Sting			

2017-2018 RINGSIDE COLLECTIBLES EXCLUSIVES		MIB	LOOSE	VALUE
2017	Chris Jericho			
	Finn Balor			
	Shane McMahon			
2018	Shawn Michaels			
	Bret Hart			
	Kurt Angle			
	Matt Hardy			
	The Brian Kendrick			
	Tyler Bate			

2019

2020

2019-2020 RINGSIDE COLLECTIBLES EXCLUSIVES		MIB	LOOSE	VALUE
2019	Jeff Hardy			
	Matt Hardy			
	The Undertaker (As Kane)			
2020	Bray Wyatt			
	Edgeheads (Edge, Zack Ryder & Curt Hawkins)			
	Walter			

2021

2022

2021-2022 RINGSIDE COLLECTIBLES EXCLUSIVES		MIB	LOOSE	VALUE
2021	Ultimate Warrior			
	John Cena			
	Cactus Jack			
	Tomasso Ciampa			
2022	The Undertaker			
	"Hollywood" Hulk Hogan			
	Cameron Grimes			
	"Macho Man" Randy Savage			
	Hulk Hogan			

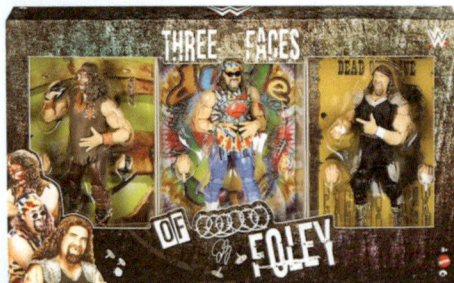 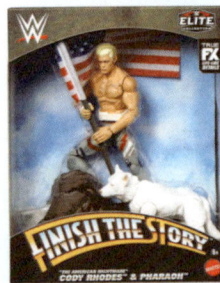

2024

2025

2023-2025 RINGSIDE COLLECTIBLES EXCLUSIVES		MIB	LOOSE	VALUE
2024	Cactus Jack			
	Dude Love			
	Mankind			
2025	Cody Rhodes			
	Pharaoh			

2024 ELITE MATTEL CREATIONS EXCLUSIVES		MIB	LOOSE	VALUE
MADE-TO-ORDER	CM Punk			
LEGENDS OF THE TERRITORY ERA	Muhammad Ali			
	Gorilla Monsoon			
	Harley Race			
	"Superstar" Billy Graham			
IMPERIUM	Giovanni Vinci			
	Ludwig Kaiser			
HEADBANGERS	Mosh			
	Thrasher			
DUDLEY BOYZ	Bubba Ray Dudley			
	D-Von Dudley			

AMAZON EXCLUSIVES		MIB	LOOSE	VALUE
2014	Mankind			
2017	Andre The Giant			
2024	Shawn Michaels			
	Razor Ramon			

GAMESTOP EXCLUSIVES		MIB	LOOSE	VALUE
2016	Brock Lesnar			
	Samoa Joe			
2017	Chris Jericho			

K-MART EXCLUSIVES		MIB	LOOSE	VALUE
2012	John Cena			

SAN DIEGO COMIC CON EXCLUSIVES		MIB	LOOSE	VALUE
2010	The Undertaker			
2016	The Shockmaster			
2017	Isaac Yankem			
2019	"Macho Man" Randy Savage			
2020	Mr. T			

WALMART EXCLUSIVES		MIB	LOOSE	VALUE
2025	John Cena (Farewell Tour)			

WWESHOP EXCLUSIVES		MIB	LOOSE	VALUE
2025	John Cena (Farewell Tour w/ Bonus Shirt)			

TARGET EXCLUSIVES		MIB	LOOSE	VALUE
2014	Rocky Maivia			
2018	The Shark			
2019	Red Rooster			

WALGREENS EXCLUSIVES		MIB	LOOSE	VALUE
2015	Shawn Michaels			
	Triple H			

TOYS 'R' US EXCLUSIVES		MIB	LOOSE	VALUE
2011	Mr. McMahon			
2012	The Undertaker			
	Triple H			
2013	Triple H			
2014	Brock Lesnar			
2015	Seth Rollins			
	John Cena			
2017	Virgil			

ALL-STARS 2-PACKS	MOC	LOOSE	VALUE
Jake "The Snake" Roberts			
Randy Orton			
"Macho Man" Randy Savage			
John Morrison			
Stone Cold Steve Austin			
CM Punk			

ELITE COLLECTION 2-PACKS 2015-2019		MIB	LOOSE	VALUE
2015 (K-MART)	Faarooq			
	The Rock			
2017 (TOYS 'R' US)	Chris Jericho			
	Kevin Owens			
2018 (WWESHOP)	Matt Hardy			
	Jeff Hardy			
2019	Jeff Hardy			
	Matt Hardy			
	AJ Styles			
	Finn Bálor			

ELITE COLLECTION 2-PACKS 2020		MIB	LOOSE	VALUE
WRESTLEMANIA MOMENT!	Rey Mysterio			
	Samoa Joe			
DX	Chyna			
	Triple H			
MONDAY NITRO	Bret "Hit Man" Hart			
	Goldberg			
WRESTLEMANIA 2	Mr. T			
	"Rowdy" Roddy Piper			

ELITE COLLECTION 2-PACKS 2021		MIB	LOOSE	VALUE
SMACKDOWN!	Triple H			
	Jeff Hardy			
ROCK 'N' SOCK	The Rock			
	Mankind			

ELITE COLLECTION 3-PACKS 2017-2019		MIB	LOOSE	VALUE
BOOTY-O'S (2017)	Big E			
	Kofi Kingston			
	Xavier Woods			
THE SHIELD (2018)	Dean Ambrose			
	Roman Reigns			
	Seth Rollins			
MILK-O-MANIA (2018)	Stephanie McMahon			
	Kurt Angle			
	Stone Cold Steve Austin			
UNDISPUTED ERA (2019)	Kyle O'Reilly			
	Adam Cole			
	Bobby Fish			

ELITE COLLECTION 3-PACKS 2022-2024		MIB	LOOSE	VALUE
HEAD OF THE TABLE VS. BEAST (AMAZON)	Brock Lesnar			
	Roman Reigns			
	Paul Heyman			
RAW 30TH (TARGET)	The Undertaker			
	Razor Ramon			
	1-2-3 Kid			
40th ANNIVERSARY OF HULKAMANIA (TARGET)	Hulk Hogan (Hulkamania)			
	"Hollywood" Hulk Hogan (nWo)			
	Hulk Hogan (Hulk Still Rules)			
MAIVIA LEGACY (WALMART)	Peter Maivia			
	The Rock			
	Rocky Johnson			
SAMOAN DYNASTY (WALMART)	Afa			
	Roman Reigns			
	Sika			
EVOLUTION (TARGET)	Batista			
	Triple H			
	Randy Orton			

ELITE COLLECTION 3-PACKS 2025-2026		MIB	LOOSE	VALUE
NEW WORLD ORDER (WALMART)	Scott Hall			
	"Hollywood" Hulk Hogan			
	Kevin Nash			
AWESOME TRUTH (TARGET)	The Miz			
	R-Truth			
	Triple H			
FAREWELL CENA (WALMART)	John Cena			
	John Cena			
	John Cena			
WYATT SICKS (WALMART)	Uncle Howdy			
	Erick Rowan			
	Nikki Cross			

ELITE COLLECTION BOXED SETS 2023-2024		MIB	LOOSE	VALUE
WWE 60TH ANNIVERSARY (TARGET)	Becky Lynch			
	Hulk Hogan			
	The Rock			
	Stone Cold Steve Austin			
THEN, NOW, FOREVER, TOGETHER (TARGET)	Becky Lynch			
	Hulk Hogan			
	The Rock			
	Stone Cold Steve Austin			
SMACKDOWN 25th ANNIVERSARY (TARGET)	Booker T			
	Stone Cold Steve Austin			
	John Cena			
	Eddie Guerrero			
LATINO WORLD ORDER (MATTEL CREATIONS)	Cruz Del Toro			
	Rey Mysterio			
	Zelina Vega			
	Santos Escobar			
	Joaquin Wilde			

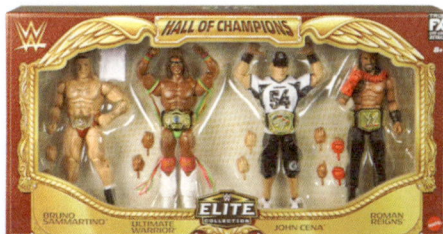

ELITE COLLECTION BOXED SETS 2025		MIB	LOOSE	VALUE
HALL OF CHAMPIONS (TARGET)	Bruno Sammartino			
	John Cena			
	Roman Reigns			
	Ultimate Warrior			

WWE LEGENDS SERIES 1

WWE LEGENDS SERIES 1	MOC	LOOSE	VALUE
Dusty Rhodes			
Ricky "The Dragon" Steamboat			
Road Warrior Animal			
Road Warrior Hawk			
Sgt. Slaughter			
Stone Cold Ateve Austin			

WWE LEGENDS SERIES 1 TAG TEAMS (TOYS 'R' US)	MOC	LOOSE	VALUE
Bushwhacker Luke			
Bushwhacker Butch			
Iron Sheik			
Nikolai Volkoff			
"Rowdy" Roddy Piper			
"Cowboy" Bob Orton			

WWE LEGENDS SERIES 2	MOC	LOOSE	VALUE
Iron Sheik			
Jake "The Snake" Roberts			
Jimmy "Superfly" Snuka			
Kamala			
"Ravishing" Rick Rude			
Terry Funk			

WWE LEGENDS HALL OF FAME (K-MART)		MOC	LOOSE	VALUE
CLASS OF 2007	"The American Dream" Dusty Rhodes			
CLASS OF 1996	Jimmy "Superfly" Snuka			
CLASS OF 2009	Ricky "The Dragon" Steamboat			
CLASS OF 2004	Sgt. Slaughter			
CLASS OF 2009	Stone Cold Steve Austin			
CLASS OF 2009	Terry Funk			

WWE LEGENDS SERIES 3	MOC	LOOSE	VALUE
Brian Pillman			
"British Bulldog" Davey Boy Smith			
"Hacksaw" Jim Duggan			
Mr. Perfect			
The Rock			
Vader			

WWE LEGENDS SERIES 4	MOC	LOOSE	VALUE
Demolition Ax			
Demolition Smash			
George "The Animal" Steele			
Hillbilly Jim			
"Mr. Wonderful" Paul Orndorff			
Ultimate Warrior			

WWE LEGENDS SERIES 5	MOC	LOOSE	VALUE
Akeem			
Bam Bam Bigelow			
"Macho Man" Randy Savage			
Rick Martel			

WWE LEGENDS SERIES 6	MOC	LOOSE	VALUE
Eddie Guerrero			
Kerry Von Erich			
Kevin Von Erich			
Texas Tornado			
Ultimate Warrior			

	WWE LEGENDS SERIES 7 (TARGET)	MIB	LOOSE	VALUE
	Bobby "The Brain" Heenan			
	Greg "The Hammer" Valentine (Black Trunks)			
CHASE	Greg "The Hammer" Valentine (Yellow Trunks)			
	Razor Ramon			

	WWE LEGENDS SERIES 8 (TARGET)	MIB	LOOSE	VALUE
	Eddie Guerrero			
	Jake "The Snake" Roberts (Maroon Tights)			
CHASE	Jake "The Snake" Roberts (Green Tights)			
	"Mr. Wonderful" Paul Orndorff			
	Ultimate Warrior			

	WWE LEGENDS SERIES 9 (TARGET)	MIB	LOOSE	VALUE
	"Million Dollar Man" Ted Dibiase (Black Suit)			
CHASE	"Million Dollar Man" Ted Dibiase (Silver Suit)			
	Nikolai Volkoff			
	Tatanka			
	The Undertaker			

	WWE LEGENDS SERIES 10 (TARGET)	MIB	LOOSE	VALUE
	Big Van Vader			
	Brutus "The Barber" Beefcake (Yellow Tights)			
CHASE	Brutus "The Barber" Beefcake (Blue Tights)			
	Diamond Dallas Page			
	John Cena			

	WWE LEGENDS SERIES 11 (TARGET)	MIB	LOOSE	VALUE
	Bam Bam Bigelow			
	Big John Studd			
	"Macho Man" Randy Savage (Pink Trunks)			
CHASE	"Macho Man" Randy Savage (Yellow Trunks)			
	Scott Hall			

	WWE LEGENDS SERIES 12 (TARGET)	MIB	LOOSE	VALUE
	Billy Gunn			
	Junkyard Dog (Red Tights)			
CHASE	Junkyard Dog (Blue Tights)			
	Kevin Nash			
	"Rowdy" Roddy Piper			

	WWE LEGENDS SERIES 13 (TARGET)	MIB	LOOSE	VALUE
	"Cowboy" Bob Orton			
	Jake "The Snake" Roberts (Blue Tights)			
CHASE	Jake "The Snake" Roberts (Grey Tights)			
	The Hurricane			
	Triple H			

	WWE LEGENDS SERIES 14 (TARGET)	MIB	LOOSE	VALUE
	Chyna			
	Edge (White Tights)			
CHASE	Edge (Red Tights)			
	"Mean" Mark Callous			
	Road Dogg			

	WWE LEGENDS SERIES 15 (TARGET)		MIB	LOOSE	VALUE
	Kane				
	Lex Luger (Black Trunks)				
CHASE	Lex Luger (Orange Trunks)				
	Stacy Kiebler				
	X-Pac				

	WWE LEGENDS SERIES 16 (TARGET)		MIB	LOOSE	VALUE
	Bradshaw				
	Faarooq				
	Molly Holly (Pink Gear)				
CHASE	Molly Holly (Blue Gear)				
	Rey Mysterio				

	WWE LEGENDS SERIES 17 (TARGET)		MIB	LOOSE	VALUE
	AJ Styles				
	Dingo Warrior				
	Ken Shamrock (Green Trunks)				
CHASE	Ken Shamrock (Blue Trunks)				
	Shawn Michaels				

	WWE LEGENDS SERIES 18 (TARGET)		MIB	LOOSE	VALUE
	Fatu (Black Tights)				
CHASE	Fatu (Floral Tights)				
	Hulk Hogan				
	Paul E. Dangerously				
	Samu (Black Tights)				
CHASE	Samu (Floral Tights)				

WWE LEGENDS SERIES 19 (TARGET)		MIB	LOOSE	VALUE
	Brother Love			
	D'Lo Brown (Nation of Domination)			
CHASE	D'Lo Brown (Black & Blue Gear)			
	Kama Mustafa			
	The Undertaker			

WWE LEGENDS SERIES 20 (TARGET)		MIB	LOOSE	VALUE
	Greg "The Hammer" Valentine			
	"Million Dollar Man" Ted Dibiase (Green Suit)			
CHASE	"Million Dollar Man" Ted Dibiase (White Suit)			
	Mr. Perfect			
	Triple H			

WWE LEGENDS SERIES 21 (TARGET)		MIB	LOOSE	VALUE
	Andre The Giant (Yellow Trunks)			
CHASE	Andre The Giant (Red Trunks)			
	Hulk Hogan			
	Iron Sheik			
	"The Mouth of The South" Jimmy Hart			

WWE LEGENDS SERIES 22 (TARGET)		MIB	LOOSE	VALUE
	Captain Lou Albano			
	Hulk Hogan (Black Knee Pads)			
CHASE	Hulk Hogan (Red Knee Pads)			
	Muhammad Ali			
	The Sultan			

WWE LEGENDS SERIES 23 (TARGET)		MIB	LOOSE	VALUE
	Big Bubba Rogers (White Shirt)			
CHASE	Big Bubba Rogers (Light Blue Shirt)			
	Hulk Hogan			
	Jamal			
	Rosey			

WWE LEGENDS SERIES 24 (TARGET)		MIB	LOOSE	VALUE
	Faarooq (Red, Yellow, Green Singlet Design)			
CHASE	Faarooq (Purple, Yellow, White Singlet Design)			
	Hulk Hogan			
	Jim "The Anvil" Neidhart			
	Kurt Angle			

WWE LEGENDS SERIES 25 (TARGET)		MIB	LOOSE	VALUE
	Bret "Hit Man" Hart			
	Justin "Hawk" Bradshaw			
	"Ravishing" Rick Rude (Numero Uno)			
CHASE	"Ravishing" Rick Rude (WCW United States Tights)			
	Sycho Sid (Blonde Hair)			
	Sycho Sid (Dark Hair)			

WWE LEGENDS SERIES 26 (TARGET)		MIB	LOOSE	VALUE
	Carlito			
CHASE	The Godfather			
	Kurt Angle			
	Rosey (Black, Red & Blue)			
CHASE	Rosey (S.H.I.T.)			

WWE LEGENDS SERIES 27 (TARGET)		MIB	LOOSE	VALUE
	Billy Gunn			
	The Great Muta			
	Terry Funk (Blue Gear)			
CHASE	Terry Funk (Red Gear)			
	Undertaker			

WWE LEGENDS SERIES 28 (TARGET)		MIB	LOOSE	VALUE
	Diesel (Diesel Power)			
CHASE	Diesel (Big "D")			
	Hunter Hearst Helmsley			
	Razor Ramon			
	Shawn Michaels			

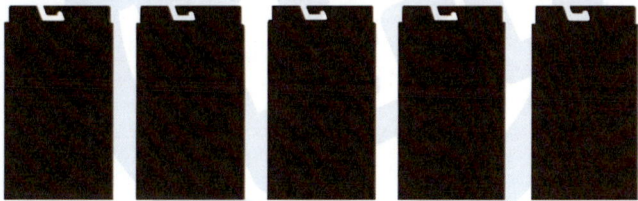

WWE LEGENDS SERIES 29 (TARGET)		MIB	LOOSE	VALUE
CHASE				

WWE LEGENDS GREATEST HITS SERIES 1		MIB	LOOSE	VALUE
LEGENDS 3	British Bulldog			
ELITE 25	Bruno Sammartino			
RETROFEST	Honky Tonk Man			
ELITE 41	Terry Funk			
FLASHBACK 1	Ultimate Warrior			

WWE LEGENDS GREATEST HITS SERIES 2		MIB	LOOSE	VALUE
ELITE 40	Irwin R. Schyster			
ELITE 14	King Booker			
ELITE 44	Tugboat			
LEGENDS 4	Ultimate Warrior			
ELITE 50	Warlord			

WWE LEGENDS GREATEST HITS SERIES 3		MIB	LOOSE	VALUE
ELITE 49	Brutus "The Barber" Beefcake			
ELITE 3	Cody Rhodes (Standard – Black Trunks)			
UNRELEASED	Cody Rhodes (Chase – Purple Trunks)			
ELITE 63	Dusty Rhodes			
TARGET EXCL.	Red Rooster			
UNRELEASED	Virgil			

WWE LEGENDS EXCLUSIVES		MOC	LOOSE	VALUE
MATTY COLLECTOR	Shawn Michaels (The Rockers)			
	Marty Jannetty (The Rockers)			
	Andre The Giant			
	Diamond Dallas Page			
	Bundy			
	Arn Anderson			
	Tully Blanchard			
RINGSIDE COLLECTIBLES	"Macho King" Randy Savage			
ULTIMATEWARRIOR.COM	Ultimate Warrior (1 of 5)			

LEGENDS INTERCONTINENTAL TITLE COMBO PACK (BASIC)	MIB	LOOSE	VALUE
The Rock			
Stone Cold Steve Austin			

ULTIMATE EDITION

ULTIMATE EDITION SERIES 1		MIB	LOOSE	VALUE
WRESTLEMANIA 34	Ronda Rousey			
WCW HALLOWEEN HAVOC 1998	Ultimate Warrior			

ULTIMATE EDITION SERIES 2		MIB	LOOSE	VALUE
WRESTLEMANIA 34	Shinsuke Nakamura			
KING OF THE RING 1994	Bret "Hit Man" Hart			

ULTIMATE EDITION SERIES 3		MIB	LOOSE	VALUE
SUMMERSLAM 2018	Finn Bálor			
SUMMERSLAM 1999	Triple H			

ULTIMATE EDITION SERIES 4		MIB	LOOSE	VALUE
SUMMERSLAM 2019	Brock Lesnar			
SURVIVOR SERIES 1997	Shawn Michaels			

ULTIMATE EDITION SERIES 5		MIB	LOOSE	VALUE
WRESTLEMANIA 35	Becky Lynch			
ROYAL RUMBLE 2008	John Cena			

ULTIMATE EDITION SERIES 6		MIB	LOOSE	VALUE
SUMMERSLAM 2018	Charlotte Flair (Ringside Collectibles)			
SURVIVOR SERIES 1998	The Rock (Amazon)			

ULTIMATE EDITION SERIES 7		MIB	LOOSE	VALUE
ROYAL RUMBLE 2020	"The Fiend" Bray Wyatt			
WCW HOG WILD 1996	"Hollywood" Hulk Hogan			

ULTIMATE EDITION SERIES 8		MIB	LOOSE	VALUE
ROYAL RUMBLE 2020	Edge			
SNME – 2/8/1992	"Macho Man" Randy Savage			

ULTIMATE EDITION SERIES 9		MIB	LOOSE	VALUE
WCW – 3/11/1989	Ric Flair			
WRESTLEMANIA 13	Stone Cold Steve Austin			

ULTIMATE EDITION SERIES 10		MIB	LOOSE	VALUE
WRESTLEMANIA 29	The Rock			
WRESTLEMANIA 22	John Cena			

ULTIMATE EDITION SERIES 11		MIB	LOOSE	VALUE
IN YOUR HOUSE: BADD BLOOD 1997	Kane			
WRESTLEMANIA XIV	The Undertaker			

ULTIMATE EDITION SERIES 12		MIB	LOOSE	VALUE
RAW – 1/18/2021	Alexa Bliss			
WRESTLEMANIA 37	"The Fiend" Bray Wyatt			

ULTIMATE EDITION SERIES 13		MIB	LOOSE	VALUE
WRESTLEMANIA	Hulk Hogan			
WRESTLEMANIA	Mr. T			

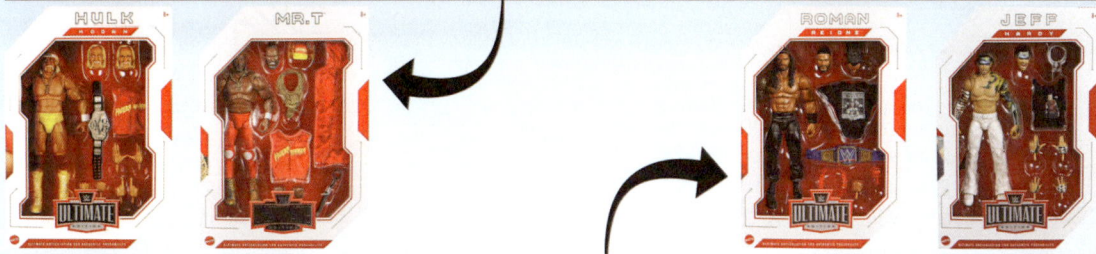

ULTIMATE EDITION SERIES 14		MIB	LOOSE	VALUE
CROWN JEWEL 2021	Roman Reigns			
RAW – 11/11/2002	Jeff Hardy			

ULTIMATE EDITION SERIES 15		MIB	LOOSE	VALUE
DAY 1	Brock Lesnar			
WRESTLEMANIA VII	Ultimate Warrior			

ULTIMATE EDITION SERIES 16		MIB	LOOSE	VALUE
WRESTLEMANIA 38	AJ Styles			
SUPERSTARS – 8/15/1992	Razor Ramon (Standard - Yellow Vest)			
SUPERSTARS – 1/8/1994	Razor Ramon (Chase - Purple Vest)			

ULTIMATE EDITION SERIES 17		MIB	LOOSE	VALUE
MONEY IN THE BANK 2022	Seth Rollins			
WRESTLEMANIA III	Andre The Giant			

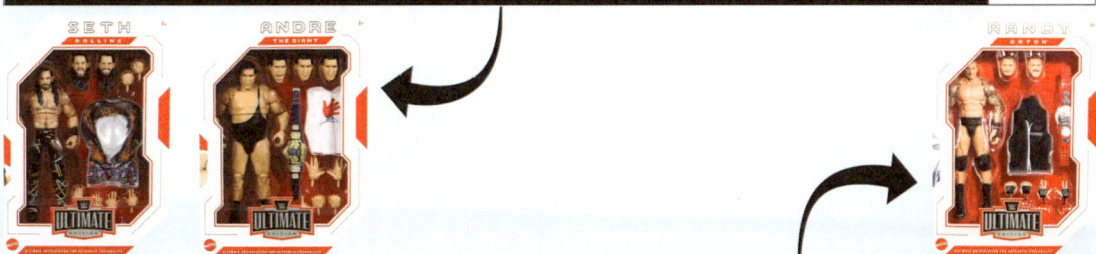

ULTIMATE EDITION SERIES 18		MIB	LOOSE	VALUE
WRESTLEMANIA 38	Randy Orton			
WRESTLEMANIA VII	"Macho Man" Randy Savage		CANCELED	

ULTIMATE EDITION SERIES 19		MIB	LOOSE	VALUE
HELL IN A CELL 2022	Bianca Belair			
CROWN JEWEL 2023	Bobby Lashley			
ROYAL RUMBLE 2001	Kurt Angle			

ULTIMATE EDITION SERIES 20		MIB	LOOSE	VALUE
ROYAL RUMBLE 2023	Asuka			
WRESTLEMANIA 39	Roman Reigns			
WRESTLEMANIA XIV	The Undertaker (Greatest Hits)			

ULTIMATE EDITION SERIES 21		MIB	LOOSE	VALUE
WRESTLEMANIA 39	Cody Rhodes			
WRESTLEMANIA 39	Kevin Owens			
WRESTLEMANIA 39	Sami Zayn			

ULTIMATE EDITION SERIES 22		MIB	LOOSE	VALUE
SUMMERSLAM 2023	Gunther			
SUMMERSLAM 2023	Jey Uso			
CROWN JEWEL 2023	John Cena			

ULTIMATE EDITION SERIES 23		MIB	LOOSE	VALUE
WRESTLEMANIA 39	Dominik Mysterio			
FASTLANE 2023	LA Knight			
WRESTLEMANIA 39	Rey Mysterio			

ULTIMATE EDITION SERIES 24		MIB	LOOSE	VALUE
ROYAL RUMBLE 2023	Bray Wyatt			
SURVIVOR SERIES 2023	Finn Bálor (Standard - White)			
ROYAL RUMBLE 2024	Finn Bálor (Chase - Black)			
SMACKDOWN – 12/8/2023	Solo Sikoa			

ULTIMATE EDITION SERIES 25		MIB	LOOSE	VALUE
MONEY IN THE BANK	Damian Priest			
GREAT AMERICAN BASH 1989	Great Muta (Standard Edition – Red)			
STARRCADE 1989	Great Muta (Chase – Black)			
WRESTLEMANIA XL	The Rock			

ULTIMATE EDITION SERIES 26		MIB	LOOSE	VALUE
WRESTLEMANIA XL	Drew McIntyre			
BACKLASH 2024	Jey Uso (White Sneakers)			
BACKLASH 2024	Jey Uso (Black Sneakers)			
ROYAL RUMBLE 2024	Jimmy Uso			

ULTIMATE EDITION SERIES 27		MIB	LOOSE	VALUE
WRESTLEMANIA XL	Bayley			
SUMMERSLAM 2024	CM Punk			
WRESTLEMANIA XL	Logan Paul			

ULTIMATE EDITION SERIES 28	MIB	LOOSE	VALUE
Eddie Guerrero			
Tiffany Stratton			
Uncle Howdy			

ULTIMATE EDITION SERIES 29		MIB	LOOSE	VALUE

ULTIMATE EDITION SERIES 30		MIB	LOOSE	VALUE

ULTIMATE EDITION SERIES 31		MIB	LOOSE	VALUE

ULTIMATE EDITION GREATEST HITS SERIES 1		MIB	LOOSE	VALUE
KING OF THE RING 1994	Bret "Hit Man" Hart			
SUMMERSLAM 1999	Triple H			

ULTIMATE EDITION GREATEST HITS SERIES 2		MIB	LOOSE	VALUE
WRESTLEMANIA 13	Stone Cold Steve Austin			
WCW HALLOWEEN HAVOC 1998	Ultimate Warrior			

ULTIMATE EDITION GREATEST HITS SERIES 3		MIB	LOOSE	VALUE
WCW HOG WILD 1996	"Hollywood" Hulk Hogan			
SUMMERSLAM 2018	Charlotte Flair			

ULTIMATE EDITION GREATEST HITS SERIES 4		MIB	LOOSE	VALUE
BACKLASH 2005	Batista (White Box)			
BACKLASH 2005	Batista (Red Box)			
SURVIVOR SERIES 1998	The Rock (White Box)			
SURVIVOR SERIES 1998	The Rock (Red Box)			

ULTIMATE EDITION GREATEST HITS SERIES 5		MIB	LOOSE	VALUE
WRESTLEMANIA III	Hulk Hogan			
MONEY IN THE BANK 2022	Seth Rollins			

ULTIMATE EDITION GREATEST HITS SERIES 6		MIB	LOOSE	VALUE
	Razor Ramon			
WRESTLEMANIA 39	Roman Reigns			

2022 ULTIMATE EDITION FAN TAKEOVER (AMAZON)		MIB	LOOSE	VALUE
WRESTLEMANIA 9	Hulk Hogan			
SMACKDOWN 12/19/08	Jeff Hardy			
WRESTLEMANIA 6	Ultimate Warrior			
SURVIVOR SERIES 2006	Triple H			
SURVIVOR SERIES 1995	Shawn Michaels			
WCW AUGUST 1998	Goldberg			

2024 ULTIMATE EDITION FAN TAKEOVER (AMAZON)	MIB	LOOSE	VALUE
Rey Mysterio			
Seth Rollins			

2025 ULTIMATE EDITION FAN TAKEOVER (AMAZON)	MIB	LOOSE	VALUE
John Cena			
Randy Orton			

2022-2023 ULTIMATE EDITION LEGENDS (TARGET)		MIB	LOOSE	VALUE
2022	Batista			
	"Macho Man" Randy Savage			
2023	Bret "Hit Man" Hart			
	The Rock			
	Ultimate Warrior			

2024 ULTIMATE EDITION LEGENDS (TARGET)		MIB	LOOSE	VALUE
	Yokozuna (Black Sarong)			
CHASE	Yokozuna (White Sarong)			
	The Undertaker			
	Dusty Rhodes			
	Vader (Black Mask)			
CHASE	Vader (Red Mask)			

2025 ULTIMATE EDITION LEGENDS (TARGET)	MIB	LOOSE	VALUE
"Hollywood" Hulk Hogan			
Shawn Michaels			
The Undertaker			
Bray Wyatt			

ULTIMATE RUTHLESS AGGRESSION 1 (WALMART)	MIB	LOOSE	VALUE
Eddie Guerrero			
Rey Mysterio			

ULTIMATE RUTHLESS AGGRESSION 2 (WALMART)	MIB	LOOSE	VALUE
Brock Lesnar			
Rob Van Dam			

ULTIMATE MONDAY NIGHT WARS 1 (WALMART)		MIB	LOOSE	VALUE
RAW	Bret "Hit Man" Hart			
NITRO	"Rowdy" Roddy Piper			

ULTIMATE MONDAY NIGHT WARS 2 (WALMART)		MIB	LOOSE	VALUE
NITRO	Eddie Guerrero			
RAW	Mankind			

2024-2025 ULTIMATE MONDAY NIGHT WAR (WALMART)		MIB	LOOSE	VALUE
RAW	Triple H			
NITRO	Lex Luger			
RAW	Stone Cold Steve Austin			
NITRO	Scott Steiner			
RAW	Kurt Angle			

ULTIMATE AMAZON EXCLUSIVES		MIB	LOOSE	VALUE
2023	Gobbledy Gooker			
	The Undertaker			
2024	Papa Shango			
	Ultimate Warrior			

ULTIMATE EDITION RINGSIDE EXCLUSIVES 2022-2023		MIB	LOOSE	VALUE
2022	Raw Ring w/ Kane			
2023	Jey Uso			
	Jimmy Uso			

ULTIMATE EDITION RINGSIDE EXCLUSIVES 2024-2025		MIB	LOOSE	VALUE
2024	Nitro Ring w/ Eric Bischoff			
	Kevin Nash			
	Scott Hall			
	Rick Steiner			
	Scott Steiner			
	CM Punk			
2025	Raw Ring w/ Rhea Ripley			
	Bubba Ray Dudley			
	D-Von Dudley			

ULTIMATE SAN DIEGO COMIC CON EXCLUSIVES		MIB	LOOSE	VALUE
2021	Sgt. Slaughter (Standard Edition – Blue Card)			
	Sgt. Slaughter (Chase Edition – Black Card)			
2022	Rip			
	Zeus			
2023	Muhammad Ali (Ring Gear)			
	Muhammad Ali (Referee)			
2024	Shawn Michaels			
2025	John Cena			

2022-2023 ULTIMATE MATTEL CREATIONS EXCLUSIVES		MIB	LOOSE	VALUE
2022	Diesel			
	Doink The Clown			
	"Macho Man" Randy Savage (1 of 8,011)			
	New Generation Authentic Scaled Ring			
	New Generation Entrance Stage			
	Wrestlmania Ring Skirts			
	In Your House Ring Skirts			
2023	Cody Rhodes			
	Logan Paul			

2025-2026 ULTIMATE MATTEL CREATIONS EXCLUSIVES		MIB	LOOSE	VALUE
2025	Cody Rhodes			
	Brandi Rhodes			
	CM Punk			

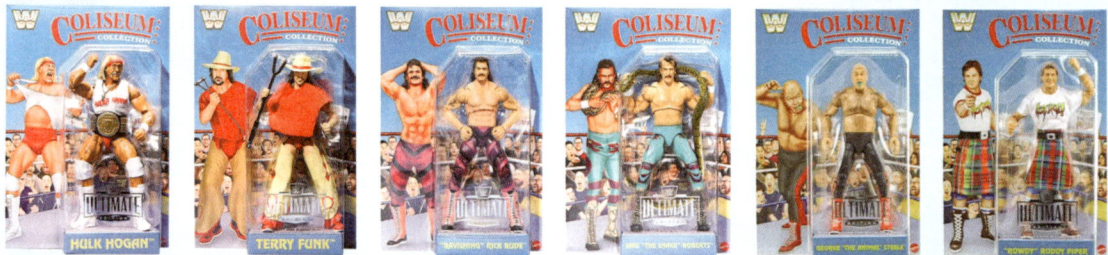

2022-2023 ULTIMATE COLISEUM COLLECTION 2-PACKS		MIB	LOOSE	VALUE
2022	Hulk Hogan			
	Terry Funk			
2023	"Ravishing" Rick Rude			
	Jake "The Snake" Roberts			
	George "The Animal" Steele			
	"Rowdy" Roddy Piper			

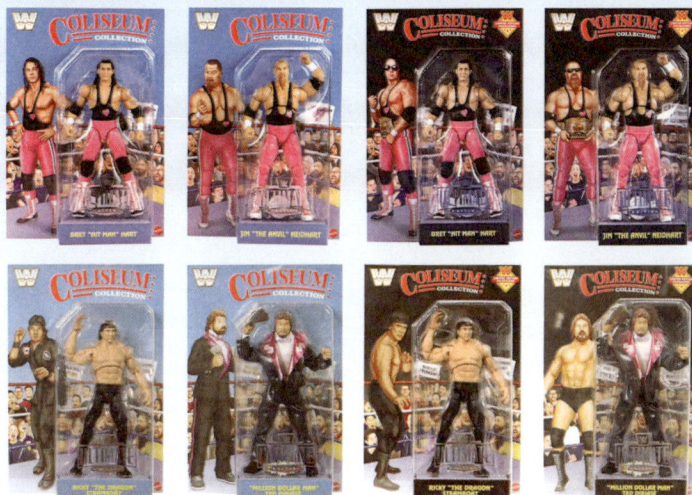

2024 ULTIMATE COLISEUM COLLECTION 2-PACKS

		MIB	LOOSE	VALUE
2024	Bret "Hit Man" Hart (Standard Edtion – Blue Card)			
	Jim "The Anvil" Neidhart (Standard Edition – Blue Card)			
	Bret "Hit Man" Hart (Chase Edtion – Black Card)			
	Jim "The Anvil" Neidhart (Chase Edition – Black Card)			
	Ricky "The Dragon" Steamboat (Standard Edtion – Blue Card)			
	"Million Dollar Man" Ted Dibiase (Standard Edition – Blue Card)			
	Ricky "The Dragon" Steamboat (Chase Edtion – Black Card)			
	"Million Dollar Man" Ted Dibiase (Chase Edition – Black Card)			

2025 ULTIMATE COLISEUM COLLECTION 2-PACKS

		MIB	LOOSE	VALUE
2025	Bam Bam Bigelow (Standard Edition – Blue Card)			
	Big Boss Man (Standard Edition – Blue Card)			
	Bam Bam Bigelow (Chase Edition – Black Card)			
	Big Boss Man (Chase Edition – Black Card)			
	Honky Tonk Man (Standard Edition – Blue Card)			
	Ultimate Warrior (Standard Edition – Blue Card)			
	Honky Tonk Man (Chase Edition – Black Card)			
	Ultimate Warrior (Chase Edition – Black Card)			

RETRO SERIES 1 (WALMART)	MOC	LOOSE	VALUE
Brock Lesnar			
John Cena ("Attitude Adustment")			
John Cena ("Attitude Adjustment")			
Kevin Owens			
Roman Reigns ("Superman Punch")			
Roman Reigns ("Super Punch")			
Ultimate Warrior			
The Undertaker			

RETRO SERIES 2 (WALMART)	MOC	LOOSE	VALUE
Kane			
Mankind			
Stone Cold Steve Austin			
Sting			
The Rock			
Triple H (1 Logo On Tights)			
Triple H (2 Logos On Tights)			

RETRO SERIES 3	MOC	LOOSE	VALUE
AJ Styles			
Dean Ambrose			
Goldberg			
Seth Rollins			

RETRO SERIES 4	MOC	LOOSE	VALUE
Finn Balor			
Kevin Owens			
Ric Flair			
Sami Zayn			

RETRO SERIES 5	MOC	LOOSE	VALUE
Big E			
Kofi Kingston			
Xavier Woods			
"Macho Man" Randy Savage (Arm Up)			
"Macho Man" Randy Savage (Arm Down)			

RETRO SERIES 6	MOC	LOOSE	VALUE
Bray Wyatt			
Daniel Bryan			
Shinsuke Nakamura			
Sting			

RETRO SERIES 7	MOC	LOOSE	VALUE
Chris Jericho			
Kurt Angle			
Shawn Michaels			
Sheamus			

RETRO SERIES 8	MOC	LOOSE	VALUE
Braun Strowman			
Iron Sheik			
Jeff Hardy			
Zack Ryder			

RETRO SERIES 9	MOC	LOOSE	VALUE
Goldust			
"Macho Man" Randy Savage			
Randy Orton			
Samoa Joe			

RETRO SERIES 10	MOC	LOOSE	VALUE
Diesel			
Elias			
Junkyard Dog			
"Woken" Matt Hardy			

RETRO SERIES 11 (MATTEL CREATIONS)	MOC	LOOSE	VALUE
"Cowboy" Bob Orton			
Mean Gene Okerlund			
Mr. T			
"Rowdy" Roddy Piper			

RETRO SERIES 12 (MATTEL CREATIONS)	MOC	LOOSE	VALUE
Bret "Hit Man" Hart			
Jim "The Anvil" Neidhart			
Jimmy Hart			
Nikolai Volkoff			

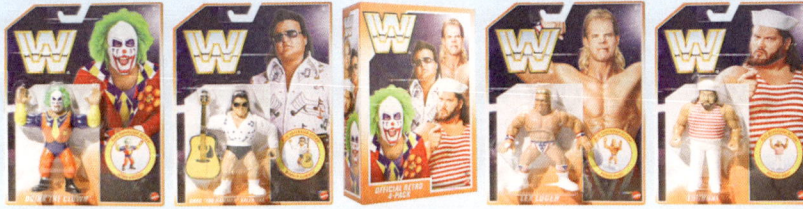

RETRO SERIES 13 (MATTEL CREATIONS)	MOC	LOOSE	VALUE
Doink The Clown			
Greg "The Hammer" Valentine			
Lex Luger			
Tugboat			

RETRO SERIES 14 (MATTEL CREATIONS)	MOC	LOOSE	VALUE
Jerry "The King" Lawler			
Paul Bearer			
The Undertaker			
Vader			

RETRO SERIES 15 (MATTEL CREATIONS)	MOC	LOOSE	VALUE
Big John Studd			
Hulk Hogan			
Muhammad Ali			
Wendi Richter			

RETRO SERIES 16 (MATTEL CREATIONS)	MOC	LOOSE	VALUE
Alundra Blayze			
British Bulldog			
Isaac Yankem			
Shawn Michaels			

RETRO SERIES 17 (MATTEL CREATIONS)	MOC	LOOSE	VALUE
Miss Elizabeth			
Rip Thomas			
Queen Sherri			
Zeus			

RETRO SERIES 18 (MATTEL CREATIONS)	MOC	LOOSE	VALUE
Bobby "The Brain" Heenan			
King Harley Race			
Ultimate Warrior			
Virgil			

RETRO SERIES 19 (MATTEL CREATIONS)	MOC	LOOSE	VALUE

RETRO SERIES 20 (MATTEL CREATIONS)	MOC	LOOSE	VALUE

RETRO NWO 2-PACKS (RINGSIDE COLLECTIBLES)	MOC	LOOSE	VALUE
Scott Hall			
Kevin Nash			
"Hollywood" Hulk Hogan			
Syxx			

RETRO DX 2-PACKS (RINGSIDE COLLECTIBLES)	MOC	LOOSE	VALUE
Chyna			
Triple H			
Billy Gunn			
Road Dogg			

RETRO BLOODLINE 2-PACKS (RINGSIDE COLLECTIBLES)	MOC	LOOSE	VALUE
Jey Uso			
Jimmy Uso			
Roman Reigns			
Solo Sikoa			

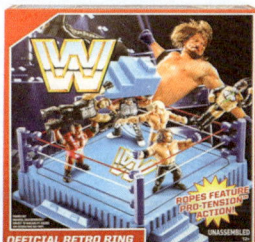

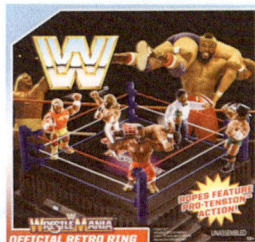

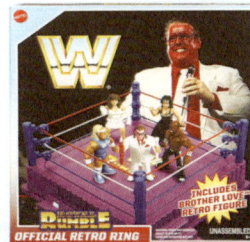

RETRO WRESTLING RINGS	MIB	LOOSE	VALUE
Official WWE Retro Ring			
Official Wrestlemania Retro Ring (Mattel Creations)			
Official Royal Rumble Retro Ring w/ Brother Love (Mattel Creations)			

MASTERS OF THE WWE UNIVERSE SERIES 1 (WALMART)	MOC	LOOSE	VALUE
Finn Balor			
Sting			
Triple H			
Ultimate Warrior			

MASTERS OF THE WWE UNIVERSE SERIES 2 (WALMART)	MOC	LOOSE	VALUE
Faker John Cena			
"Macho Man" Randy Savage			
Rey Mysterio			
Roman Reigns			

MASTERS OF THE WWE UNIVERSE SERIES 3 (WALMART)	MOC	LOOSE	VALUE
Braun Strowman			
The New Day (Big E Face Showing)			
The New Day (Kofi Kingston Face Showing)			
The New Day (Xavier Woods Face Showing)			
The Rock			
The Undertaker			

MASTERS OF THE WWE UNIVERSE SERIES 4 (WALMART)	MOC	LOOSE	VALUE
"The Fiend" Bray Wyatt			
Jake "The Snake" Roberts			
Mr. T			
Seth Rollins			

MASTERS OF THE WWE UNIVERSE SERIES 5 (WALMART)	MOC	LOOSE	VALUE
Becky Lynch			
"Macho Man" Randy Savage			
Ricky "The Dragon" Steamboat			
"Rowdy" Roddy Piper			

MASTERS OF THE WWE UNIVERSE SERIES 6 (WALMART)	MOC	LOOSE	VALUE
Goldberg			
Kane			
Stephanie McMahon			
Ultimate Warrior			

MASTERS OF THE WWE UNIVERSE SERIES 7 (WALMART)	MOC	LOOSE	VALUE
Andre The Giant			
Bret "Hitman" Hart			
Junkyard Dog			
Sgt. Slaughter			

MASTERS OF THE WWE UNIVERSE SERIES 8 (WALMART)	MOC	LOOSE	VALUE
Stone Cold Steve Austin			
Chyna			
Rey Mysterio			

MASTERS OF THE WWE UNIVERSE RINGS (WALMART)	MIB	LOOSE	VALUE
Grayskull Ring			
Grayskull Mania (w/ Triple H & John Cena)			
Rattlesnake Mountain (w/ Stone Cold Steve Austin & Hulk Hogan)			

WWE SUPERSTARS SERIES 1 (WALMART)	MOC	LOOSE	VALUE
Bray Wyatt			
"Hollywood" Hulk Hogan			
Honky Tonk Man			
Ric Flair			

WWE SUPERSTARS SERIES 2 (WALMART)	MOC	LOOSE	VALUE
Kevin Nash			
Scott Hall			
Shawn Michaels			
Ultimate Warrior			

WWE SUPERSTARS SERIES 3 (WALMART)	MOC	LOOSE	VALUE
Mankind			
"Million Dollar Man" Ted Dibiase			
Papa Shango			
The Undertaker			

WWE SUPERSTARS SERIES 4 (WALMART)	MOC	LOOSE	VALUE
"Macho Man" Randy Savage			
Mr. T			
The Rock			
Typhoon			

WWE SUPERSTARS SERIES 5 (WALMART)		MOC	LOOSE	VALUE
Earthquake				
"Macho Man" Randy Savage				
"Ravishing" Rick Rude				
The Rock				

WWE SUPERSTARS SERIES 6 (WALMART)		MOC	LOOSE	VALUE
	Bam Bam Bigelow			
	Hulk Hogan (Red & Yellow)			
CHASE	Hulk Hogan (Blue & White)			
	Mr. Perfect			
	"Rowdy" Roddy Piper			

WWE SUPERSTARS SERIES 7 (WALMART)		MOC	LOOSE	VALUE
	Captain Lou Albano			
	Hulk Hogan (Red & Yellow)			
CHASE	Hulk Hogan (Blue & White)			
	"Rowdy" Roddy Piper			
	Vader			

WWE SUPERSTARS SERIES 8 (WALMART)		MOC	LOOSE	VALUE
	Andre The Giant			
	Doink The Clown			
	Hulk Hogan (Red Tights)			
CHASE	Hulk Hogan (Blue Tights)			

WWE SUPERSTARS SERIES 9 (WALMART)		MOC	LOOSE	VALUE
	British Bulldog			
	Kane			
	Muhammad Ali			

WWE SUPERSTARS SERIES 10 (WALMART)		MOC	LOOSE	VALUE
	Big Boss Man			
	Kurt Angle			
	Tatanka			

WWE SUPERSTARS SERIES 11 (WALMART)		MOC	LOOSE	VALUE
	Brutus "The Barber" Beefcake			
	Razor Ramon (Blue Gear)			
CHASE	Razor Ramon (Purple Tights)			
	Rey Mysterio Jr.			

WWE SUPERSTARS SERIES 12 (WALMART)		MOC	LOOSE	VALUE
	Bret "Hit Man" Hart			
	Cactus Jack			
	Jim "The Anvil" Neidhart			

	WWE SUPERSTARS SERIES 13 (WALMART)	MOC	LOOSE	VALUE
	Eddie Guerrero			
	Jake "The Snake" Roberts (Green Tights)			
CHASE	Jake "The Snake" Roberts (White Tights)			
	Ricky "The Dragon" Steamboat			

	WWE SUPERSTARS SERIES 14 (WALMART)	MOC	LOOSE	VALUE
	Diesel			
	The Great Muta (Red Pants)			
CHASE	The Great Muta (Black Pants)			
	Iron Sheik			
	Zeus			

WWE SUPERSTARS SERIES 15 (WALMART)	MOC	LOOSE	VALUE
George "The Animal" Steele			
Nikolai Volkoff			
Stone Cold Steve Austin			
Ultimate Warrior			

WWE SUPERSTARS SERIES 16 (WALMART)	MOC	LOOSE	VALUE
The Hurricane			
Rick Steiner			
Rob Van Dam			
Scott Steiner			

WWE SUPERSTARS SERIES 17 (WALMART)	MOC	LOOSE	VALUE

WWE SUPERSTARS SERIES 18 (WALMART)	MOC	LOOSE	VALUE

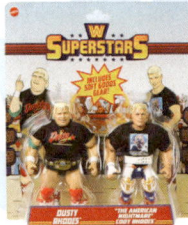

WWE SUPERSTARS 2-PACKS (MATTEL CREATIONS)	MOC	LOOSE	VALUE
Cody Rhodes			
Dusty Rhodes			

CREATE-A-WWE-SUPERSTAR SERIES 1	MIB	LOOSE	VALUE
Bray Wyatt			
Hulk Hogan			
John Cena			
Kane			
Randy Orton			
Sheamus			
Stone Cold Steve Austin			
The Rock			

CREATE-A-WWE-SUPERSTAR DELUXE SERIES 1		MIB	LOOSE	VALUE
Gladiator Set	Triple H			
Lucha Set	Rey Mysterio			
Martial Arts Set	Seth Rollins			
Rocker Set	Kane			
Special Ops Set	Roman Reigns			
Zombie Set	The Undertaker			

CREATE-A-WWE-SUPERSTAR 2-PACK	MIB	LOOSE	VALUE
John Cena			
Triple H			

CREATE-A-WWE-SUPERSTAR SERIES 2	MIB	LOOSE	VALUE
John Cena			
Goldust			
Rusev			
Ultimate Warrior			

CREATE-A-WWE-SUPERSTAR DELUXE SERIES 2		MIB	LOOSE	VALUE
Enforcer Set	Dean Ambrose			
Gladiator Set	Triple H			
Hip Hop Set	John Cena			
Shadow Vigilante Set	Sting			
Special Ops Set	Roman Reigns			

TOUGH TALKERS SERIES 1	MIB	LOOSE	VALUE
Bray Wyatt			
Dean Ambrose			
John Cena			
Kevin Owens			
Roman Reigns			
Seth Rollins			

TOUGH TALKERS SERIES 2	MIB	LOOSE	VALUE
Big E			
Brock Lesnar			
Dean Ambrose			
John Cena			
Kofi Kingston			
Xavier Woods			

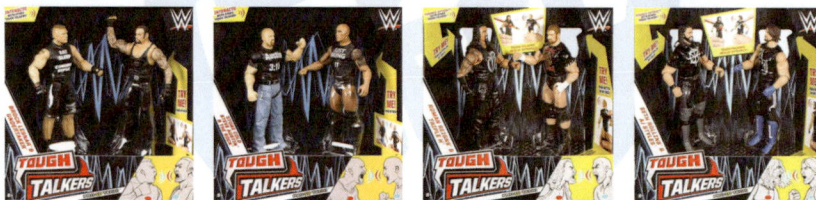

TOUGH TALKERS 2-PACKS	MIB	LOOSE	VALUE
Brock Lesnar			
The Undertaker			
Stone Cold Steve Austin			
The Rock			
Roman Reigns			
Triple H			
Seth Rollins			
AJ Styles			

TOUGH TALKERS HALL OF FAME (TARGET)	MIB	LOOSE	VALUE
"Macho Man" Randy Savage			
Ric Flair			
"Rowdy" Roddy Piper			

TOUGH TALKERS: TOTAL TAG TEAM SERIES 1	MIB	LOOSE	VALUE
AJ Styles			
Big Cass			
Enzo Amore			
Finn Balor			
John Cena			
Randy Orton			
Sami Zayn			
Sting			
The Undertaker			
Xavier Woods			
Big E			
Kofi Kingston			
Kevin Owens			
Chris Jericho			

SOUND SLAMMERS SERIES 1	MIB	LOOSE	VALUE
Dean Ambrose			
John Cena			
Kevin Owens			
Roman Reigns			
Seth Rollins			

SOUND SLAMMERS SERIES 2	MIB	LOOSE	VALUE
AJ Styles			
Bobby Roode			
Finn Balor			
Kurt Angle			
The Miz			

SOUND SLAMMERS SERIES 3	MIB	LOOSE	VALUE
Bobby Roode			
Cesaro			
Finn Balor			
Seth Rollins			
"Woken" Matt Hardy			

SOUND SLAMMERS SERIES 4	MIB	LOOSE	VALUE
Randy Orton			
Roman Reigns			
Sheamus			
The Rock			

WREKKIN' 2019 ASSORTMENT	MIB	LOOSE	VALUE
AJ Styles			
John Cena			
Seth Rollins			
The Miz			
The Undertaker			
"Woken" Matt Hardy			

WREKKIN' 2020 ASSORTMENT	MIB	LOOSE	VALUE
Daniel Bryan			
Elias			
Finn Balor			
John Cena			
Kofi Kingston			
Randy Orton			
Rey Mysterio			
Ricochet			
Roman Reigns			
Seth Rollins			
The Miz			
The Rock			
Triple H			
The Undertaker			

WREKKIN' 2021 ASSORTMENT	MIB	LOOSE	VALUE
Drew McIntyre			
John Cena			
Randy Orton			
Roman Reigns			
Seth Rollins			
The Rock			
Triple H			
The Undertaker			

BEND 'N' BASH SERIES 1	MIB	LOOSE	VALUE
John Cena			
Rey Mysterio			
Roman Reigns			
The Rock			

BEND 'N' BASH SERIES 2	MIB	LOOSE	VALUE
Bobby Lashley			
Drew McIntyre			
Kofi Kingston			
The Undertaker			

BEND 'N' BASH SERIES 3	MIB	LOOSE	VALUE
Big E			
Damian Priest			
Rey Mysterio			
Seth Rollins			

BEND 'N' BASH DELUXE PACKS	MIB	LOOSE	VALUE
John Cena			
Roman Reigns			

POWER SLAMMERS SERIES 1	MIB	LOOSE	VALUE
John Cena (Green)			
Randy Orton			
Rey Mysterio (Yellow)			
Sheamus			

POWER SLAMMERS SERIES 2	MIB	LOOSE	VALUE
Alberto Del Rio			
Brodus Clay			
Kofi Kingston			
The Miz			
Zack Ryder			

POWER SLAMMERS SERIES 3	MIB	LOOSE	VALUE
Kane			
Santino Marella			
Sin Cara			
The Rock			

POWER SLAMMERS 2-PACKS SERIES 1	MIB	LOOSE	VALUE
John Cena			
Randy Orton			
Rey Mysterio (Black)			
Sheamus			

POWER SLAMMERS 2-PACKS SERIES 2	MIB	LOOSE	VALUE
CM Punk			
Kane			
John Cena (Blue)			
The Rock			

BRAWLIN' BUDDIES SERIES 1		MIB	LOOSE	VALUE
	John Cena (Camo)			
	Randy Orton			
	Rey Mysterio (Green)			
WALMART	Rey Mysterio (Red)			
	Sheamus			

BRAWLIN' BUDDIES SERIES 2	MIB	LOOSE	VALUE
Kofi Kingston			
Rey Mysterio (Blue)			
Zack Ryder			

BRAWLIN' BUDDIES 2-PACKS (TOYS 'R' US)		MIB	LOOSE	VALUE
BUDDIES	John Cena (Jorts)			
	Rey Mysterio (Green)			
CHAMPIONS	Ryback			
	John Cena			

CHAMPIONSHIP BRAWLIN' BUDDIES		MIB	LOOSE	VALUE
	Brodus Clay			
	John Cena			
TOYS 'R' US	Ryback			
	Sheamus			
	The Rock			

3-COUNT CRUSHERS	MIB	LOOSE	VALUE
John Cena			
Roman Reigns			
Seth Rollins			
The Rock			

12" 2013 ASSORTMENT	MIB	LOOSE	VALUE
Albertio Del Rio			
John Cena			
Kane			
Sheamus			
Sin Cara			

12" 2014 ASSORTMENT	MIB	LOOSE	VALUE
John Cena			
Kane			
Sheamus			

12" 2015 ASSORTMENT	MIB	LOOSE	VALUE
John Cena			
Sin Cara (Purple)			
Sin Cara (Yellow)			
The Rock			

12" 2017 ASSORTMENT	MIB	LOOSE	VALUE
Brock Lesnar			
Brock Lesnar (T-Shirt)			
Dean Ambrose			
Finn Balor			
Finn Balor (T-Shirt)			
John Cena (Blue Wrist Bands)			
John Cena (Orange Wrist Bands)			
John Cena (Red & Blue Wrist Bands)			
Kalisto			
Roman Reigns			
Seth Rollins			
Seth Rollins (T-Shirt)			
Sting			
Stone Cold Steve Austin			
The Rock			
The Rock (T-Shirt)			
Triple H			
Triple H (T-Shirt)			

TRUE MOVES SERIES 1	MIB	LOOSE	VALUE
AJ Styles			
Daniel Bryan			
Kalisto			
Kane			
Kevin Owens			
Kurt Angle			
Randy Orton			
Seth Rollins			

TRUE MOVES SERIES 2	MIB	LOOSE	VALUE
Bruan Strowman			
Bray Wyatt			
Cesaro			
Gran Metalik			
Kane			
Kevin Owens			
Randy Orton			
The Undertaker			

TRUE MOVES SERIES 3	MIB	LOOSE	VALUE
Jeff Hardy			
Rey Mysterio			

TRUE MOVES MAIN EVENT SET	MIB	LOOSE	VALUE
Kane			
The Undertaker			
John Cena			
Daniel Bryan			

WOMEN'S SUPERSTARS FASHIONS 12" DOLLS	MIB	LOOSE	VALUE
Alicia Fox			
Asuka			
Bayley			
Becky Lynch			
Carmella			
Charlotte Flair			
Eva Marie			
Lana			
Natalya			

WOMEN'S SUPERSTARS FASHIONS DELUXE 12" DOLLS	MIB	LOOSE	VALUE
Alexa Bliss			
Bayley			
Becky Lynch			
Brie Bella			
Charlotte Flair			
Naomi			
Natalya			
Nikki Bella			
Ronda Rousey			
Sasha Banks (Blue Dress)			
Sasha Banks (Green Dress)			

WOMEN'S SUPERSTARS FASHIONS 12" DOLLS MULTIPACKS		MIB	LOOSE	VALUE
5-PACK	Natalya			
	Becky Lynch			
	Sasha Banks			
	Brie Bella			
	Nikki Bella			
CANADA EXCLUSIVE 5-PACK	Becky Lynch			
	Charlotte Flair			
	Stephanie McMahon			
	Sasha Banks			
	Bayley			
SDCC 2017	Charlotte Flair			
	Sasha Banks			

WOMEN'S SUPERSTARS 6" ACTION FIGURES	MOC	LOOSE	VALUE
Alexa Bliss			
Brie Bella			
Becky Lynch			
Charlotte Flair			
Naomi			
Natalya			
Nikki Bella			

WOMEN'S SUPERSTARS MISCELLANEOUS RELEASES		MOC	LOOSE	VALUE
ULTIMATE FAN PACKS	Bayley			
	Bayley (w/ DVD)			
	Charlotte Flair			
	Sasha Banks			
	Sasha Banks (w/ DVD)			
TAG TEAM SUPERSTARS	Bayley			
	Becky Lynch			
	Sasha Banks			
PLAYSETS	Ultimate Entrance Playset (w/ Nikki Bella)			

2011 WWE RUMBLERS SINGLES ASSORTMENT	MOC	LOOSE	VALUE
Big Show			
CM Punk			
Edge			
Evan Bourne			
John Cena (Purple Wrist Bands, No Hat)			
John Cena (Purple Wrist Bands w/ Hat)			
John Cena (Orange Wrist Bands w/ Hat)			
John Morrison			
Kane			
Kofi Kingston			
Randy Orton			
Rey Mysterio (Black)			
Rey Mysterio (Blue)			
Rey Mysterio (Red)			
Sheamus			
The Miz			
Triple H			
The Undertaker			

2011 WWE RUMBLERS 2-PACK ASSORTMENT	MOC	LOOSE	VALUE
Alberto Del Rio			
Rey Mysterio (Black)			
Big Show			
Rey Mysterio (White)			
Big Show			
Triple H			
CM Punk			
R-Truth			
Drew McIntyre			
The Undertaker			
Edge			
Randy Orton			
Evan Bourne (Red Tights)			
John Morrison (Black Pants)			
Evan Bourne (Black Tights)			
The Miz (Blue Trunks)			
Goldust			
Kofi Kingston (Yellow Trunks)			
Hornswoggle			
John Cena (Purple Wrist Bands w/ Hat)			
Jack Swagger			
John Cena (Purple Wrist Bands, No Hat)			
John Cena (Orange Wrist Bands w/ Hat)			
Sheamus			
John Cena (Purple Wrist Bands w/ Hat)			
Wade Barrett			
Kane			
Rey Mysterio (Blue & Yellow)			
Kofi Kingston (Blue Trunks)			
Justin Gabriel			
Rey Mysterio (Red)			
John Morrison (Silver Pants)			
Santino Marella			
John Morrison (Black Pants, Red Boots)			
Sheamus			
Randy Orton			
The Great Khali			
Hornswoggle			
The Miz (Red Trunks)			
Kofi Kingston (Green Trunks)			
Triple H			
Shawn Michaels			
The Undertaker			
Mark Henry			

2011 WWE RUMBLERS MULTIPACKS		MOC	LOOSE	VALUE
3-PACKS (WALMART)	Kofi Kingston			
	Rey Mysterio			
	John Morrison			
	Sheamus			
	John Cena			
	Triple H			
BATTLE ROYAL 7-PACK (TOYS 'R' US)	CM Punk			
	Kofi Kingston			
	The Undertaker			
	John Cena			
	Triple H			
	JohnMorrison			
	Rey Mysterio			

2011 WWE RUMBLERS PLAYSETS	MOC	LOOSE	VALUE
Blast & Bash Battle Ring (w/ John Cena & Sheamus)			
Steel Cage (w/ Rey, Cena, Undertaker, Big Show, Triple H & Sheamus)			
Casket Match Playset (w/ The Undertaker)			
Entrance Blast Playset (w/ John Morrison)			
Ladder Match Playset (w/ John Morrison)			
Ringside Takedown Playset (w/ Randy Orton)			
Smack Attack Playset (w/ The Miz)			
Spinshot Ladder Playset (w/ Edge)			
Steel Cage (w/ Rey Mysterio)			
TitanTron Tower (w/ Evan Bourne)			
Rumblers Ring (w/ Rey Mysterio & Kane)			
Transforming Rumble Rig (w/ Rey Mysterio)			

2012 WWE RUMBLERS SINGLES ASSORTMENT	MOC	LOOSE	VALUE
Alberto Del Rio			
Big Show			
CM Punk			
John Cena (Navy Wrist Bands)			
John Cena (Red Wrist Bands)			
Kofi Kingston			
Randy Orton			
Rey Mysterio			
Sin Cara			
The Rock			
Triple H			
The Undertaker			
Wade Barrett			

2012 WWE RUMBLERS 2-PACK ASSORTMENT	MOC	LOOSE	VALUE
Alex Riley			
The Miz			
Brodus Clay			
Alberto Del Rio			
Christian			
Alberto Del Rio			
CM Punk			
John Cena			
Cody Rhodes			
Rey Mysterio			
Daniel Bryan			
Sheamus			
Evan Bourne			
Dolph Ziggler			
John Cena (T-Shirt)			
Randy Orton			
John Cena (Red Hat)			
The Rock			
Justin Gabriel			
Exekiel Jackson			
Kane			
The Undertaker			
Mason Ryan			
Big Show			
Rey Mysterio (Gold & Silver)			
Jack Swagger			
R-Truth			
Jack Swagger			
Sheamus			
Christian			
Sin Cara			
Evan Bourne			
The Miz			
Randy Orton			
Zack Ryder			
Rey Mysterio			

2012 WWE RUMBLERS MISCELLANEOUS RELEASES		MIB	LOOSE	VALUE
BATTLE ROYAL 7-PACK	Big Show			
	The Miz			
	Randy Orton			
	John Cena			
	Rey Mysterio			
	Sheamus			
	Ezekiel Jackson			
APPTIVITY	CM Punk			
	John Cena			
	Mark Henry			
	Randy Orton			
	Rey Mysterio			
	Sheamus			
APPTIVITY 2-PACK	John Cena			
	Sin Cara			
APPTIVITY 3-PACK	Rey Mysterio			
	John Cena			
	Randy Orton			

2012 WWE RUMBLERS PLAYSETS	MIB	LOOSE	VALUE
Aerial Battle Playset (w/ Randy Orton)			
Attack Pack (w/ John Cena & The Miz)			
Attack Pack (w/ Rey Mysterio & R-Truth)			
Climb & Crash Playset (w/ Kofi Kingston)			
Flip-Out Ring Playset (w/ John Cena)			
Crash Cage Playset (w/ Kane)			
Crash Cage Playset (w/ Randy Orton)			
Ringing Entrance Playset (w/ Rey Mysterio)			
Slam Cam Playset (w/ Rey Mysterio)			
WWE Championship Playset (w/ Triple H)			
World Heavyweight Championship Playset (w/ Rey)			
World Heavyweight Championship Playset (w/ Orton)			
WWE Championship Playset (w/ John Cena)			
United States Championship Playset (w/ Kofi Kingston)			
Forklift Smashdown Playset (w/ John Cena)			
Launchin' Limo Playset (w/ Alberto Del Rio)			
Slambulance Playset (w/ Sheamus)			
Money In The Bank Playset (w/ The Miz)			
Rumblers Ring (w/ John Cena & The Miz)			
Rumblers Ring (w/ Alberto Del Rio & Rey Mysterio)			
Blastin' Breakdown Playset (w/ Alberto Del Rio & Cena)			
Ring Gift Set (w/ 10 Rumblers)			

2013 WWE RUMBLERS 2-PACK ASSORTMENT	MOC	LOOSE	VALUE
Antonio Cesaro			
Brodus Clay			
Big Show			
John Cena			
Booker T			
Cody Rhodes			
Brock Lesnar			
John Cena			
CM Punk			
Kane			
Hunico			
Rey Mysterio			
"Macho Man" Randy Savage			
CM Punk			
R-Truth			
The Miz			
Ryback			
Rey Mysterio			
Stone Cold Steve Austin			
The Rock			
Tensai			
Justin Gabriel			
The Rock			
Triple H			
Ultimate Warrior			
Sheamus			
Yoshi Tatsu			
Zack Ryder			

2013 WWE RUMBLERS MULTIPACKS		MIB	LOOSE	VALUE
ROYAL RUMBLE 7-PACK (TOYS 'R' US)	Kane			
	Big Show			
	Rey Mysterio			
	John Cena			
	Randy Orton			
	Kofi Kingston			
	Sheamus			

2013 WWE RUMBLERS RAMPAGE	MOC	LOOSE	VALUE
Brock Lesnar			
CM Punk			
John Cena (Power Punch)			
John Cena (Super Jump)			
Kane			
Kofi Kingston			
Randy Orton			
Rey Mysterio (Blue)			
Rey Mysterio (White)			
Sheamus			
Sin Cara (Red)			
Sin Cara (White)			
The Undertaker			
Zack Ryder			

2013 WWE RUMBLERS RAMPAGE PLAYSETS	MIB	LOOSE	VALUE
Crash Pack Playset (w/ John Cena)			
Crash Pack Playset (w/ Sheamus)			
Crash Cage Playset (w/ John Cena & The Rock)			
Ladder Battle Playset (w/ Randy Orton & Mark Henry)			
Scaffold Smash Playset (w/ The Miz & Kofi Kingston)			
Devastadium (w/ Rey Mysterio)			
Transforming Tour Bus (w/ The Rock)			

WWE RUMBLERS EXCLUSIVES		MIB	LOOSE	VALUE
SDCC 2011	The Rock			
SDCC 2012	Rey Mysterio			
SDCC 2013	The Miz			
ROAD TO WM XXVIII	John Cena			
	The Rock			

SLAM CITY SERIES 1	MOC	LOOSE	VALUE
Alberto Del Rio			
Big Show			
Brock Lesnar			
John Cena			
Kane			
Rey Mysterio			

SLAM CITY SERIES 2	MOC	LOOSE	VALUE
Daniel Bryan			
Stone Cold Steve Austin			
The Undertaker			

SLAM CITY 2-PACKS SERIES 1	MOC	LOOSE	VALUE
CM Punk			
The Miz			
John Cena			
Dolph Ziggler			
Sheamus			
Wade Barrett			

SLAM CITY 2-PACKS SERIES 2	MOC	LOOSE	VALUE
Damien Sandow			
Alberto Del Rio			
Dolph Ziggler			
Randy Orton			
Brock Lesnar			
Mark Henry			

SLAM CITY 2-PACKS SERIES 3	MOC	LOOSE	VALUE
Randy Orton			
Santino Marella			
Sheamus			
Brock Lesnar			

SLAM CITY PLAYSETS & EXCLUSIVES		MIB	LOOSE	VALUE
4-PACK	Sheamus			
	Rey Mysterio			
	John Cena			
	Randy Orton			
PLAYSETS	Blast'N Smash Cart (w/ CM Punk)			
	Breakdown Assault Vault (w/ The Finisher)			
	Gorilla In The Cell Match (w/ Randy Orton & Gorilla)			
	Launch'N Crash Car (w/ John Cena)			
SDCC 2014	John Cena			

MIGHTY MINIS SERIES 1		MIB	LOOSE	VALUE
CHASE	Bret Hart (Blue)			
	Bret Hart (Pink)			
	Daniel Bryan			
	Dolph Ziggler			
	John Cena			
	Roman Reigns			
	Rusev			
	Seth Rollins			
	Ted Dibiase			
	The Undertaker			

MIGHTY MINIS SERIES 2		MIB	LOOSE	VALUE
	Brock Lesnar			
	Dean Ambrose			
	Goldust			
	John Cena			
	Kane			
	Stone Cold Steve Austin			
	The Rock			
	Triple H			
CHASE	Ultimate Warrior (White)			
	Ultimate Warrior (Orange)			

MIGHTY MINIS EXCLUSIVES & PLAYSETS		MIB	LOOSE	VALUE
RINGS	Portable Mini Ring (w/ Roman Reigns & Seth Rollins)			
	Portable Mini Ring (w/ Roman, Cena, HHH, Rock & Brock)			
EXCLUSIVES	Dean Ambrose (SDCC)			

BEAST MODE SERIES 1	MIB	LOOSE	VALUE
AJ Styles			
Becky Lynch			
Braun Strowman			
Daniel Bryan			
Finn Balor			
Roman Reigns			
The Rock			
Triple H			

BEAST MODE SERIES 2	MIB	LOOSE	VALUE
Becky Lynch			
Big E			
Bray Wyatt			
Kofi Kingston			
Seth Rollins			
The Rock			
The Undertaker			
Xavier Woods			

	MISCELLANEOUS MINI FIGURES	MIB	LOOSE	VALUE
MICRO SERIES 1	The Rock			
	John Cena			
	Finn Balor			
	Roman Reigns			
	AJ Styles			
MICRO SERIES 2	Braun Strowman			
	The Undertaker			
	The Rock			
	John Cena			
	AJ Styles			
FLEXTREMES	John Cena			
	The Rock			
	Roman Reigns			
	Finn Balor			

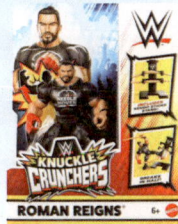

KNUCKLE CRUNCHERS SERIES 1	MIB	LOOSE	VALUE
John Cena			
Roman Reigns			
Seth Freakin' Rollins			
The Rock			

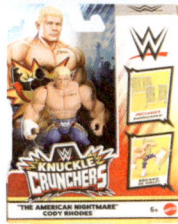

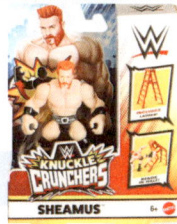

KNUCKLE CRUNCHERS SERIES 2	MIB	LOOSE	VALUE
Bobby Lashley			
Cody Rhodes			
Sheamus			
Stone Cold Steve Austin			

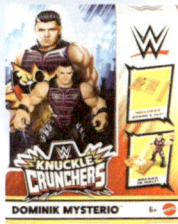

KNUCKLE CRUNCHERS SERIES 3	MIB	LOOSE	VALUE
AJ Styles			
Dominik Mysterio			
John Cena			
Rey Mysterio			

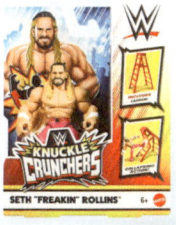

KNUCKLE CRUNCHERS SERIES 4	MIB	LOOSE	VALUE
Damian Priest			
Finn Bálor			
The Rock			
Seth Freakin' Rollins			

KNUCKLE CRUNCHERS SERIES 5	MIB	LOOSE	VALUE
Cody Rhodes			
Jey Uso			
Jimmy Uso			
Roman Reigns			

KNUCKLE CRUNCHERS SERIES 6	MIB	LOOSE	VALUE
Drew McIntyre			
John Cena			
Rey Mysterio			
Undertaker			

KNUCKLE CRUNCHERS SERIES 7	MIB	LOOSE	VALUE
CM Punk			
"Dirty" Dominik Mysterio			
LA Knight			
Stone Cold Steve Austin			

KNUCKLE CRUNCHERS RINGS & PLAYSETS	MIB	LOOSE	VALUE
Rebound Ring (w/ Brock Lesnar)			
Rebound Ring (w/ Seth Rollins)			
Rebound Ring (w/ Cody Rhodes, Seth Rollins, John Cena & Roman Reigns)			
Final Boss Microphone Playset (w/ The Rock)			

2010-2011 WRESTLING RINGS & PLAYSETS		MIB	LOOSE	VALUE
	ECW Superstar Ring			
TOYS 'R' US	Elimination Chamber			
	Elite Scale Ring			
	Raw Superstar Ring			
	Raw Superstar Ring (w/ John Cena & Big Show)			
	Ringside Battle Playset			
	Smackdown Superstar Ring			
K-MART	Steel Cage Match (w/ John Cena & Randy Orton)			
WALMART	Steel Cage Match (w/ John Cena & The Miz)			
K-MART	Tables, Ladders & Chairs Playset			
TOYS 'R' US	Wrestlemania Superstar Ring			

2012 WRESTLING RINGS & PLAYSETS		MIB	LOOSE	VALUE
K-MART	Backstage Brawl Playset			
TOYS 'R' US	Money In The Bank Playset (w/ Dolph Ziggler)			
K-MART	Raw Superstar Entrance Stage			
WALMART	Ringside Battle Playset (w/ John Cena & Alberto Del Rio)			
	Smackdown Superstar Ring			
	Steel Cage Accessory			
	Summerslam Superstar Ring			
K-MART	Survivor Series Superstar Ring			
	The Cell Playset			
K-MART	Tribute To The Troops Ring			
TOYS 'R' US	Wrestlemania Superstar Ring (w/ John Cena & The Rock)			
	Wrestlemania Superstar Ring (w/ Triple H & The Undertaker)			

2013-2014 WRESTLING RINGS & PLAYSETS		MIB	LOOSE	VALUE
	Behind The Scenes Brawl			
TOYS 'R' US	Money In The Bank Playset (w/ Seth Rollins)			
	Raw Superstar Ring			
TOYS 'R' US	Ringside Battle Playset (w/ Daniel Bryan)			
	Ringside Mayhem Accessory Set			
	Royal Rumble Superstar Ring			
	Smackdown Superstar Ring			
	Steel Cage Accessory			
	Summerslam Superstar Ring			
	The Cell Playset			
K-MART	Tornado Tag Team (w/ Goldust, Stardust, Mizdow & Miz)			
K-MART	Training Center Takedown			
	Ultimate Entrance Stage			
TOYS 'R' US	Wrestlemania Superstar Ring (w/ Brock Lesnar & Roman Reigns)			

2015-2016 WRESTLING RINGS & PLAYSETS		MIB	LOOSE	VALUE
SMYTHS	WWE Crash Cage			
	Classic Steel Cage Playset (w/ Rick Rude & Ultimate Warrior)			
	Contract Chaos (w/ Finn Bálor)			
	Money In The Bank Playset (w/ Seth Rollins)			
	NXT Superstar Ring			
	Raw Superstar Ring			
SMYTHS	Ringside Battle Playset (w/ Kevin Owens)			
	Smackdown Superstar Ring			
SMYTHS	WWE Crash Cage (w/ Triple H)			

2017-2018 WRESTLING RINGS & PLAYSETS		MIB	LOOSE	VALUE
SMYTHS	Contract Chaos (w/ AJ Styles)			
	Contract Chaos (w/ Sheamus)			
	Crash Cage (w/ AJ Styles)			
	Elimination Chamber (w/AJ Styles)			
	Money In The Bank (w/ Dean Ambrose)			
	NXT Ring			
TARGET	NXT Takeover Ring (w/ Finn Bálor)			
TOYS 'R' US	Ringside Mayhem			
	Raw Main Event Ring (w/ Goldberg)			
	Raw Ring 2017			
	Raw Ring 2018			
SMYTHS	Ringside Battle (w/ Finn Bálor)			
	Smackdown Main Event Ring (w/ Jinder Mahal)			
	Smackdown Live Ring			
TARGET	WCW Wing (w/ Dusty Rhodes)			
	Wrestlemania Ring			
TOYS 'R' US	Wrestlemania Superstar Ring (w/ The Rock & Triple H)			
TOYS 'R' US	Wrestlemania Superstar Ring (w/ John Cena & The Undertaker)			
	Wrestlemania 34 Ring (w/ Randy Orton)			
	WWE Live Ring			

2019-2020 WRESTLING RINGS & PLAYSETS		MIB	LOOSE	VALUE
ARGOS	Contract Chaos (w/ John Cena)			
	Raw/Survivor Series Superstar Ring			
	Smackdown Live/Royal Rumble Superstar Ring			
	Wrestlemania/Summerslam Superstar Ring			
SMYTHS	Wrestlemania 36 Ring (w/ John Cena & Bray Wyatt)			

2021-2023 WRESTLING RINGS & PLAYSETS		MIB	LOOSE	VALUE
	NXT Superstar Ring 2021			
	Raw Superstar Ring 2021			
	Smackdown Superstar Ring 2021			
	Wrestlemania Superstar Ring (w/ The Rock & John Cena)			
	Raw Superstar Ring 2022			
	Smackdown Superstar Ring 2022			
TARGET	WWE Legends Classic Ring			

2024-2025 WRESTLING RINGS & PLAYSETS	MIB	LOOSE	VALUE
	Money In The Bank Cash-In Ring			
	Survivor Series War Games Ring (w/ Randy Orton)			
SMYTH'S	Wrestlemania XL Ring (w/ The Rock & Roman Reigns)			

MEET THE AUTHOR

Fig Heel is a self-proclaimed Professional Wrestler Collector, Author, TikToker, YouTuber and overall content creator with over 200,000 social media followers. With over 35 years of collecting under his belt, Fig Heel has amassed over 10,000 pieces from all decades and eras of wrestling as well as a vast knowledge on the hobby.

In 2023, Fig Heel teamed up with WWE Superstar Xavier Woods to compete in Wheel of Fortune's Tournament of Champions for Wrestlemania 39. Soon after, he accomplished a lifetime goal of releasing his own action figure, hosted the now defunct Case Fresh Podcast alongside Fig Vault and soon launching his own clothing line!

Other works include The Unreleased Wrestling Figure Coloring Book series and The Ultimate Wrestling Figure Checklist series which is an Amazon.com number 1 Bestseller! When not figure hunting and adding to his collection, he enjoys bodybuilding, graphic design and spending time with family, friends and his girlfriend Macho Fran.

FOLLOW FIG HEEL ON SOCIAL MEDIA @FIGHEEL

MEET THE PHOTOGRAPHER

Matthew Goldberg is a photographer, videographer, brand ambassador, avid wrestling action figure collector and former collectibles columnist for WrestleZone.com, just to name a few.

Matt has created animated videos for World Wrestling Entertainment, Inc. and was the former studio photographer for All Elite Wrestling's Jazwares action figure and toy line. He is also the founder of Wrestling Figure News Source (@WrestleFigNews) on X and his work was recently featured in the May 2023 issue of Pro Wrestling Illustrated as well.

You may have seen his work over the years featured by Mattel, Ringside Collectibles, TNA Impact, Jakks Pacific and many other worldwide brands!. When not producing content for brands and entertainment companies, he likes to produce imagery and videos on his social media pages.

FOLLOW MATTHEW ON SOCIAL MEDIA @MBG1211

265

www.ingramcontent.com/pod-product-compliance
Ingram Content Group UK Ltd.
Pitfield, Milton Keynes, MK11 3LW, UK
UKRC030740131125
8879UKWH00030B/99

9 798898 601539